MODELING JESUS

Walking Single-Minded in a Double-Minded World

BRAD CLIMER

My daughter Emilie
My son Braden

His Outpouring Church Family – You are a light in my life. Thank you
for letting me be your pastor.

SPECIAL THANKS

Karen Duval – Thank you for editing a bit and lots of feedback. And, the encouragement.

John Onorato – Thank you for the encouragement and helping with this book. We have navigated the publishing waters together.

CONTENTS

PREFACE

I remember a conversation with a friend in 2017 like it took place only ten minutes ago. Previously, I had been an excited, sold-out, prophetic teacher who was "hearing God." I traveled, ministered, and experienced God's presence with miracles. But when I talked with this friend, that was a distant memory that seemed like years ago.

I had experienced defeat in my Christian walk. There was no joy, no happiness, and no real desire to serve God anymore. I had wandered "in the desert" for many years. I had once lived in the joy of the Lord, but now I vaguely remembered what I considered the "goodness of God."

There had been tragedies: a divorce, a fiancée who died suddenly, and a child struggling with drugs while living on the street. The "church talk" just didn't fit me anymore. It wasn't authentic to me. It seemed Christians were all "parroting" each other. I wanted out of the crazy. No more. I was done! I was doing my best to simply maintain. I didn't want to experience anymore hurt. I couldn't. I *wouldn't*.

My friend said to me, "What you miss is the time with your Father."

Those words pierced my heart. I had heard the truth. I was

on my knees asking God to restore—but restore what? I was okay with Him. At least I repeated that over and over. I was trying to convince myself, but I knew it wasn't true. I was incredibly offended. Offended by God. Mad because I felt misunderstood. I didn't even understand myself. I had given all I had to serve Him, and now I felt like I'd been cast aside.

My real struggle came when I had to talk to the Christian world. I couldn't handle the Christian atmosphere the way it was presented. It seemed insincere. I felt no one heard me. I was unsafe...judged. I actually told our Father that I would see Him in forty years when I died. I wanted to go to heaven, but I no longer had the stamina to run the race on this earth.

As I was on my knees, Father said the most-interesting thing to me: "I want you to go to Wyoming and start an outpouring."

Excitement filled my soul. *How do I do that?* I wondered. *And why in the world Wyoming?* Even so, I did it. This was the beginning of a journey that would change my life. It would bring me to a place of certainty, confidence, abiding, and, best of all, *knowing* I was in God's will.

It became my *single-minded* purpose. It became my place of stability.

Later, I heard a prophet of God that many in the body of Christ esteemed highly (he has since gone to heaven). While I was viewing an old clip of his preaching, he made a statement that rang true to the very depths of my spirit: he spoke of the difference between the fivefold ministry gifts that Jesus offers (Ephesians 4:11–13) and the "spirit of religion" the church has left us with.

The fivefold ministry to equip the body of Christ are: 1) apostles, 2) prophets, 3) evangelists, 4) teachers, and 5) pastors. These gifts are to mature us so we become faith-and-love beings, as Jesus was. With faith and love we are able to do the works of the ministry, which are soul-winning, healing the sick, visiting orphans and widows, and being about our Father's business.

This prophet also spoke of the "spirit of religion" and the five gifts it has left the church:1) legalism, 2) opinion, 3) debate, 4) criticism, and 5) judgment. Upon hearing that powerful statement, I had a moment of clarity—and a moment of profound sadness.

The body of Christ has severely limited itself by not operating in a *single-minded* fashion, which is to love our neighbor. I've seen how the body of Christ has again restrained itself by not single-mindedly obeying our Father's instructions for His church. I've seen Christians thrown into continual drama (like the world!) while the lost and the dying don't have the gospel preached to them.

My prayer for us as we read this book is simple: I want us to fall in love with our Father. I want us to honor and follow Him. I want us to fall so in love with Him that His opinion matters more than anyone else's, even our own. I want us to fall in love with our Father to the point that we prefer our neighbor more than we do ourselves. In other words, we do as Jesus did, which was doing what the Father told Him to do.

The byproduct of this is that we love God, we love others, and we love ourselves. The drama in the church and in our lives will then melt away. Instead of being about our own business, we are now about our Father's business. This is my simple prayer.

INTRODUCTION

Jesus modeled a perfect life for us in this world. He is our example. His life was so simple that following Heavenly Father was his only reality. He overcame the world by keeping His focus on the will of His Father and not on the problems that He faced. Jesus was single-minded to that task.

He was single-focused on why He came to this earth. His task was to seek and save those who were lost (Luke 19:10). Jesus, by His example, demonstrated that we can also follow through with Holy Spirit's instructions single-mindedly. Scripture tells us "as he is, so are we in this world" (1 John 4:17). And if He modeled this for us, we can obviously model it too. Why else would He have said we could be like Him in this world?

Jesus dealt with the daily issues of life, just like we do. He continually contended with the attacks of the religious system, and at times was mobbed by people who wanted a miracle or pressed by those looking for an answer. Consider the crowds He fed, the storms He overcame, those who betrayed Him, and the sheer number of people His ministry touched on a day-to-day basis. Pressing needs and issues filled His days, and He handled each one with kindness and compassion.

There is no life situation we will face that Jesus hasn't already experienced—and not only experienced, but overcome. That makes the concept of being single-minded, like He was, so important for us.

I find that staying focused on the things Holy Spirit tells us, is the safest way for us to live. It is the place of our security. Consider this: Could the loss of focus on the instructions of Holy Spirit be the "sin that so easily besets us" described in Hebrews 12:1? Could this be where we forget what Holy Spirit has said to us? When we stop being single-minded to heavenly instructions, are we now in a double-minded world of sin, fear, and doubt? Doesn't the Bible say that "whatever is not from faith is sin" (Romans 14:23)?

There is a place of acting and not reacting to the struggles life throws at us, and of getting a proactive answer from God. It is called being single-minded. This mindset brings the reality of light and life into our world. This way of living becomes the reality, instead of the darkness, fear, doubt, sin, and self-sufficiency many live in now. We allow Holy Spirit to take control, and finally let go of our problems and learn how to trust.

The double-minded life will always be one of doubt and second-guessing. We were not put on this earth to be defeated; we were put here to walk with our Creator. We are to learn to live single-mindedly, just as Jesus did. We are to overcome the world by single-minded action, to be everything we were created to be, and to reach our full potential. Jesus lived a hundredfold life. Since He did it, it's possible for us too. The Creator did not intend for us to live a defeated life. We were created to attain all of God's treasures.

When we don't follow His instructions, it keeps us from entering into His blessings. Never quite walking all the way in. We stop when it gets hard. We stop when we don't see the way out of our situation anymore. We stop because we have lost sight of our first love (see Revelation 2:4). We stop because it is no longer fun.

It is possible to live the divine, single-minded life, because we are told that "as He is, so are we in this world" (1 John 4:17). The *He* in that verse is our Savior. That's enough for me. Is it enough for you? We were put on this earth to affect a dying and lost world. Can we go do that? Can we walk in that treasure room? Can we be the "light of the world" and the "city set on a hill" (Matthew 5:14)? Or are we doomed to live in drama and defeat? Instead of doing the will of our Father, are we going to be caught up in defeat, anxiety, and self-centeredness? Have a life similar to what the world lives?

No, thank you!

So let's find out about this single-minded life. Let's discover our Father's design for walking in it. We are not alone in this life; Father is here to guide us every step of the way and give us a life of peace—a life in His perfect will.

SINGLE- VERSUS DOUBLE-MINDEDNESS

A s we begin this book, I'm asking you to think in a fresh, new way. I'm asking you to let Holy Spirit show you something new—or maybe not new but undiscovered. Something hidden that can be found. Some have it and walk in it. Others feel it and own it. Many don't even know it's there. But what if we take an old truth and give it a fresh perspective? That's all I ask as you read this book.

The Bible contains a significant parable whose opening verse Jesus points to as the key to understanding and discovering the Word in a fresh way. It's a concept. A truth. "Then Jesus said to them, 'If you can't understand the meaning of this parable, how will you understand all the other parables?'" (Mark 4:13 NLT).

This is a pivotal statement, a benchmark of understanding Scripture. What is contained in this parable? What happens when we understand it? Jesus emphasized that we need to understand it so we know it's possible.

Jesus had to have a good reason for pointing us here. This parable must hold a key to how we're to function in the kingdom. In His kingdom. Therefore, not understanding what's being said in Scripture is no longer an option. It should never be an option. We should always seek to understand it.

If we don't understand what Scripture is saying, we can be double-minded to His will and instructions. He states that we won't understand other parables if we don't understand this one. We should know what our Father wants us to do in this life. Being double-minded to His will greatly contributes to our lack of clarity, and the clarity that comes when we understand Scripture is paramount to having a victorious life. When we understand what is being said, we can now consider it. When we are able to consider, we can then choose. When we choose to follow Holy Spirit, we learn to overcome. And overcoming is how we want to live in this life.

This parable is a frequently preached, debated, understood, *and* misunderstood passage. Of course it is. The deep things of God have to be sought, discovered, and mined. They are a mystery until they become a reality, and the realities are the foundations from which we build our faith.

This parable of the sower and the seed can also be found in Matthew 13 and Luke 8. Since Jesus called it the key to the kingdom, let's investigate.

When I read this passage of Scripture, my eyes opened to the rest of the Bible in a fresh and living way. I saw for the first time how Jesus modeled Himself for the disciples—for us—and why He operated the way He did. Suddenly I understood why Paul made statements like "I press toward the mark for the prize of the high calling of God in Christ Jesus" (Philippians 3:14 KJV). I understood how he abandoned his life to follow Christ because he believed that obeying and honoring God was the highest calling for his life.

I have often wondered how men like Smith Wigglesworth, Charles Finney, George Mueller, and John Wesley were able to stay so focused and committed to God. They were men who were set like flint (see Isaiah 50:7) regarding the call burning in their hearts. Forsaking all, they followed Christ. They *lived* the gospel instead of just *talking* about it. They considered it an honor to abandon this world and fall in love with their Savior.

They were single-minded. Why has the modern Christian community not burned as brightly as these men did?

Jesus states in John 14:12, "Most assuredly, I say to you, he who believes in Me, the works that I do he will do also; and greater works than these he will do because I go to My Father" (NKJV). This is another verse that's debated and interpreted in a variety of ways. But it seems that Paul duplicated, to a great degree, what Jesus modeled. If you consider the revelation Paul wrote, the miracles he operated in, and the churches he planted, it is clear that he knew the importance of operating single-mindedly. Paul said, "Follow me as I follow Christ" (1 Corinthians 11:1 MEV).

Being single-minded is a major truth contained in the gospel. Single-minded to what? To what God instructs (we will study this in more detail in the parable of the sower and the seed in chapter 2). Many wonderful teachers have taught us that we must live by faith. When we make faith statements and carefully craft prayers but choose to live, talk, and walk the way we want, things don't work out. Something is missing.

Mark 4 provides a path for us so we can choose to be an overcomer. Everything we need to overcome is in this parable. It shows us how we can learn to access faith the way Jesus did. He modeled a faith that never failed, by walking in the Spirit. Since He is our example and Holy Spirit is our Help and Comforter, we're assured that it's possible.

Perhaps denominational interpretation has caused this parable to get lost in the modern church. Perhaps our personal interpretations muddy the simplicity of it. The fact that we have more sickness than ever before, more children addicted to drugs, and a crisis of identity in our world tells us that we're not focused the way Jesus was; it's double-mindedness on our part. Now more than ever is the time to learn what is in this bold parable. I love my Savior and His boldness.

If ever there was a time for strong, committed followers of Christ, it's now. There has to be more. We can feel it in our bones. We can and should be operating as Jesus did. That's still possible. I will never be convinced otherwise. We need to take our society back. We need revival.

I have dealt with sickness, addiction, and crisis of identity in my own family. Many times I've asked God why change isn't happening. Why aren't more people getting free? Why are we not doing it the way Jesus did? I wasn't accusing. I just wanted clarification. The Lord said that He will never leave us nor forsake us (Deuteronomy 31:6), so I know He wants us to be single-minded to His promises. He wants us to overcome. He wants our faith strengthened. He wants us to walk as Jesus did on this earth—a place of great faith and great answers. A place where Jesus is truly Lord. Where the whole Godhead is involved. "This is the victory that overcometh the world, even our faith" (1 John 5:4 KJV).

Let's look at Mark 4:13 and explore how being single-minded puts us into a position to receive the way Jesus did.

THE PARABLE OF THE SOWER

The parable of the sower is found in Mark 4, Matthew 13, and Luke 8. It speaks of seeds, birds, types of soil, and hearing. It also details everything needed to understand and interpret the mystery that is referred to in Mark 4:13: "If you can't understand the meaning of this parable, how will you understand all the other parables?" (NLT).

Not only do we want an understanding of this parable, but we also need insight on how to apply it in our lives. Remember, Jesus expressed it as being a pivotal revelation. Understanding this opened a fresh understanding of the entire Bible for me, and I want to share it with you.

THE SEED

Mark 4:3: "Give attention to this! Behold, a sower went out to sow."

Jesus's Explanation: "The sower sows the word" (Mark 4:14).

The "seed" that is sown is a seed of instruction from Holy Spirit to us. It's a personal word for us to observe and follow. This would be a *rhema* word, defined as "God's word spoken to

you." Holy Spirit is speaking to us. It could be a specific assignment, the answer to a problem, an idea for a business, something
to start/stop doing in our lives, or instructions for how to treat
an individual. We are told to do something by God.

For those who are new to it, the most effective way to hear
God is through His Word. Simply find a passage in the Bible
that meets the criteria for solving our problem. Examples could
be the answer to our current dilemma, how to handle our children, how to conduct ourselves morally, how to get physical healing, etc. The passage we discover becomes our seed. Holy Spirit
speaks through it, honors it, and makes us overcomers by it.

Consider 1 Peter 2:24 for physical healing: "By [Jesus']
wounds you have been healed." This is the perfect Scripture to
stand on for healing of physical infirmity. It is a *logos* word—a
promise we take from the Bible. When we find a Bible promise
that is the solution to the problem we're facing, we can stand on
it. That promise becomes a personal word for our lives. The
Bible was written for us, so it's important that it becomes
personal to us. Remember, God's Word is His will.

God delivers His truths to us in seed form. He speaks to us.
We are responsible for making sure this life-giving seed becomes
a strong plant. Truth in our lives. That is our job. We are to use
our God-given will and follow through on the instructions our
Father gives us. We are to resolve to faint not. To continue on in
God and the assignment He has given us.

We can have as much of God as we want. He has no shortage
of seeds, and He isn't intimidated by the problems we face. It's
important to secure a word from Him—a seed, if you will. Let's
now discover the soil.

THE SOIL

We are "the soil" described in this parable. It is our soul—our
mind, will, and emotions. The way we think. How we react to
situations and processes in daily life. What we will or won't do.

What we believe. What we stand for. How we handle happiness and stress. How we look at a problem, how we process instruction, and how we function.

Our Father plants a seed, in the form of words or instructions, into the soil: us. In John 10:27, Jesus says, "My sheep hear my voice" (KJV). The seed is planted when we hear God's instructions. He is the Creator of all life. He is bringing life into our situation. He is our Comforter here to help us. However, now the onus is on us. We've heard from Him, so we're responsible for what we do with that seed. It's our job to care for that instruction with a single-minded focus—to not let it die. It dies because we become double-minded by focusing on the world.

Now let's consider the soil types. The soil represents our mindset, or the types of attitudes people have toward God's instructions.

Hardened Path

Mark 4:4: "And as he was sowing, some seed fell along the path, and the birds came and ate it up."

Jesus's Explanation: "The ones along the path are those who have the Word sown [in their hearts], but when they hear, Satan comes at once and [by force] takes away the message which is sown in them" (Mark 4:15).

This is a well-worn path, a patch of soil that has been trodden down by constant foot traffic. The seed has a greatly limited ability to grow and germinate here. This type of soil (mindset), therefore, has a greatly limited potential to hear. The instructions of Father are severely hindered. This mind is not open to God because of life experiences that reinforce defeat. The path has been tread upon to the extent that the hardened ground will not allow the seed to take root easily, and the seed is lying on top of the ground. To make matters worse, the birds (the demons sent by the Enemy) come and eat it.

The strongholds, or systems of thought, in this mindset, are so ingrained that it's hard to receive from God. Anything Holy Spirit says is barely considered. One could call this a closed mind or a mind that has little hope. A mind that struggles to contemplate or hear another point of view. Life has literally beaten down this soil. Without hope the heart is sick (see Proverbs 13:12). This is a defeated place.

Stony Soil

Mark 4:5: "Other seed [of the same kind] fell on ground full of rocks, where it had not much soil; and at once it sprang up, because it had no depth of soil; And when the sun came up, it was scorched, and because it had not taken root, it withered away."

Jesus's Explanation: "And in the same way the ones sown upon stony ground are those who, when they hear the Word, at once receive and accept and welcome it with joy" (Mark 4:16).

This type of soil (mindset) has the potential to hear but carries a contrary system of thought. In other words, it hears and considers for a while, but the preconceived ideas win out. The systems of thought that have always been there are the rocks that limit the growth of the seed (or the instructions given).

Jesus stated that the stony soil provided limited room for the roots to grow, and these roots are the beginning of obedience. The plant grows for a short time until the sun (or life's resistance) scorches the plant. It doesn't have an adequate root system to withstand the sun or the contrary evidence disputing what has been instructed. The strong preconceived ideas are the stones in our hearts that cause death to the emerging plant (or to our Father's instructions to us). The possibility of a heavenly resolution is terminated by preconceived ideas that cause a lack of depth in our soil.

One example would be a person who accepts Jesus as their Lord and Savior but returns to their old way of life. This person is initially excited to be a born-again Christian, but the lure of sin and sensual excitement wins out, so the evidence of a victorious life goes latent. This is similar to someone wanting to quit smoking cigarettes. They try to "willpower it," but the desire and habit of smoking win out. The victory of kicking the habit is gone.

Consider a believer who has had a disagreement with another Christian. They hear a "seed" taught about not taking offense and forgiving your brother. They decide, "Everything is okay. Let's just put it behind us." Later, something triggers the memory of the offense and they become angry with that person again. They are still offended even though they tried to make amends.

I really like how this is described in Proverbs 17:9: "Overlook an offense and bond a friendship; fasten on to a slight and—good-bye, friend!" (MSG). The seed of not being offended, which had begun to grow into a seedling, withers and dies. Another great example of rocky soil would be the prophet Jonah, who will be discussed in chapter 6.

Thorny Soil

Mark 4:7: "Other seed [of the same kind] fell among thorn plants, and the thistles grew and pressed together and utterly choked and suffocated it, and it yielded no grain."

Jesus's Explanation: "Then the cares and anxieties of the world and distractions of the age, and the pleasure and delight and false glamour and deceitfulness of riches, and the craving and passionate desire for other things creep in and choke and suffocate the Word, and it becomes fruitless" (Mark 4:19).

"Cares" (v. 19) could be defined as double-minded. The Greek defines it as dividing or fracturing into parts. Either persecution or pleasure can cause our soul realm to not fulfill its potential. A deeper understanding of what takes place in this mindset is that other things in our lives have a priority over the instructions given to us by our Father. We get caught up in life, and the instructions (or the seed) given to us by our Father get overruled. We are divided between our "life" situations and our Holy Spirit instructions. We weren't meant to handle life's situations by ourselves. He wants to be our help "in time of need" (Hebrews 4:16 NKJV), and desires to walk with us at all times.

We want to follow our Father, we really do. However, cares of life such as lack of money, concern over our children, greed, health issues, opinions of others, etc., become a priority in our lives. We attempt to meet our needs and desires without considering what God offers us in His Word.

Worrying about our needs being met is larger, in our mind, than "my God shall supply all your need according to His riches in glory by Christ Jesus" (Philippians 4:19 NKJV). We take this Scripture and quote it, meditate on it, and pray it. But the concern and worry gradually overwhelm us. We haven't made a decision to let this seed (Scripture) grow in our thinking. Our mind is not renewed to His financial provision. Now the thorns start to choke our plant. We look at our checkbook balance, we see no raise at our job, and we can't make the house payment on time. We stand for a while, but our mind becomes divided and we lose our faith. We know our problems better than we know our Father's guidance.

Simply put, "the lust for other things" are the decisions that take priority in our lives. We forget God's instructions because we want to go our own way. We don't prioritize our lives to honor His Word. We decide we want life on our terms instead. It seems like a good idea to let the seed germinate in our thinking, but we default to our lusts and conclusions and end up going our own way. We are like the person who looks in a mirror and walks off and forgets what they look like (see James 1:23). This is double-minded. Remember, God's instructions are always designed to further His kingdom, not to further *us* in His kingdom.

Enough of the negative scenarios. Let's look at good soil and a single-minded mindset that wants to honor God by following His instructions.

Good Soil

Mark 4:8: "And other seed [of the same kind] fell into good (well-adapted) soil and brought forth grain, growing up and increasing, and yielded up to thirty times as much, and sixty times as much, and even a hundred times as much as had been sown."

Jesus's Explanation: "And these are they which are sown on good ground; such as hear the word, and receive it, and bring forth fruit, some thirtyfold, some sixty, and some a hundred" (Mark 4:20).

Good soil! This is a mindset that wants to follow Holy Spirit's instructions, a mindset that will prioritize its life to attain holy direction. We can have our life affected thirtyfold (30 percent) by these instructions, we can have our life affected sixtyfold (60 percent) by these instructions, or we can have our life affected one hundredfold (100 percent) of these instructions.

One hundred percent is the realm Jesus walked in and He intends us to walk in. He said, "I do nothing of Myself; but as My Father taught Me, I speak these things" (John 8:28 NKJV). This is where true faith comes into play. A single-minded mindset is determined to follow God at all costs and regardless of the outcome. It's a mindset that wants to please the Father because we know He is a better guide than our mind and experience are. This is a place of strength but also utter dependence on Him. We leave the land of winning and losing based upon what we see in this earthly realm, and fellowship and following His direction become the ultimate reward. This is where the full reward "well done, good servant" (Luke 19:17 NKJV) is attained.

This is where I personally missed it, as mentioned in the preface. I was so hurt and disillusioned by the Christian walk—and by Christians in general—that I was no longer following our

Father's instructions for my life. I was too deep in my own double-mindedness of pain, grief, and opinion. I wanted to go to heaven, but I didn't want to deal with God's instructions. That, my friend, is delusion.

And yet, many Christians today live like this. They never consult or talk with God. I can't live that way, and I hope you can't either.

God healed me over time. It took a while, but He is good at that. I started listening to Him again. I slowly started to trust Him again. He had never failed me, but the Christian world had. I quit blaming Him for their decisions concerning me. I let only *His* opinion of me matter again. Slowly, tediously, and *finally*, I trusted Him one more time.

I'm glad I did. Now I can't imagine my day without our Father. I wake up thinking about Him and go to bed thinking about Him. I'm restored and whole. I'm single-minded again, choosing to walk 100 percent.

Let's now look at what the birds signify in this parable.

THE BIRDS

Mark 4:4: "And as he was sowing, some seed fell along the path, and the birds came and ate it up."

Jesus's Explanation: "The ones along the path are those who have the Word sown [in their hearts], but when they hear, Satan comes at once and [by force] takes away the message which is sown in them" (Mark 4:15).

The birds are agents of Satan—demons. They are most active on the hardened path, the person who has allowed issues and problems to overtake their life. The seed will ultimately grow, even on a hardened path, as long as the birds don't come and eat it. Remember, the seeds sown are the instructions of God. If that instruction can find a crack in the path, it will grow. Satan doesn't want that to happen, so he sends the birds (demons). These demons try to reinforce the stronghold in our thinking by stealing the seed. The answer is stolen, and we don't embrace the change.

The Enemy doesn't want us single-minded. He wants us to be double-minded and caught in the problem. He wants us to never see a solution. To say, "My life will never change." Even though promises like "I can do all things through [Christ]" (Philippians 4:13) are powerful and life-changing, the demons, coupled with double-minded thinking, keep this person captive.

Now we can see why intercessors help people get unstuck and out of hard circumstances. Through their prayers, they stand against the demons. People with this mindset are so overcome by their problems that the Enemy has a field day eating God's attempts to restore them.

Finally, let's look at the element of hearing in this parable.

HEARING

Mark 4:9 says, "And He said, He who has ears to hear, let him be hearing [and let him consider, and comprehend]."

I like what this verse is saying. We have spiritual ears and the ability to hear God. We're able to consider what Holy Spirit is saying to us. We not only need to hear Him but also consider what He is telling us. This is the "thinking it through" stage. From here we can comprehend what we're hearing or reading.

Comprehension is huge. This is where we make our stand and own what we believe. It's the place of being unshakable when contrary circumstances try to thwart what we now see as truth. His truth. Bible truth. Our life truth contained in Scripture.

Real faith takes place—the faith to step up and do what is being presented to us. The faith to take a Scripture and give it preeminence in our life. To let the seed, given to us by our Father, be more real than our life circumstances, no matter what the problem or situation we face.

We are able to change the soil in our life. We can go from

stony soil or thorny soil, to good soil. We can take that seed, the instruction given to us, and move it to better soil. And remember, Holy Spirit will never leave us nor forsake us. He says that if we lack wisdom, He will give us all the help we need. He will help us move our seed to the right soil, and help us get our soil ready to receive seed. And He will give the instruction to us by His Spirit, a Scripture, or an unction.

Isn't this the grace that's so misunderstood? It's all by grace. That's not for debate. But by understanding this parable, we come to understand our Father's heart toward us—a heart that wants none to perish (see 2 Peter 3:9). Grace is God's ability to work in us so we can do what we can't do in our own ability.

The person who takes the seed, plants it in the right soil, and nurtures and cares for it, has a harvest. We hear it and walk out those instructions single-mindedly, and we can now expect a solution because keeping His instructions is all we focus on.

Those who are able to hear will be given more. They are growing in hearing His instructions, and in the ability to follow Scripture instead of giving in to circumstances. They are beginning to be trusted by Heavenly Father, so they are moving into a position to receive more.

Now let's look at some examples of the many places where single-minded obedience is shown in the Bible. Since there are so many, we'll look at three in particular.

ALL THROUGH THE BIBLE

We can see the blessings of being single-minded all through Scripture. There are many examples—too many to cover in this book—so I've chosen a few to illuminate the blessings of single-mindedness.

ADAM AND EVE

From Adam and Eve in Genesis, all the way to the book of Revelation, the theme that always comes up is that God's way with single-minded resolve will always be the best choice. It will always be the way He intended us to live from the beginning. The alternative to ignoring this truth is we fall into double-minded folly by choosing to go our own way.

The story of Adam and Eve is one that ends with great sadness, but it is also one of learning to overcome. There's more to the story than just the eating of the forbidden fruit. It's a story of *not* following God's single- minded instruction that leads to blessings and instead traveling a double-minded path that leads to destruction and a defeated life.

And the Lord God took the man and put him in the Garden of Eden to tend and guard *and* keep it. And the Lord God commanded the man, saying, You may freely eat of every tree of the garden; But of the tree of the knowledge of good and evil *and* blessing and calamity you shall not eat, for in the day that you eat of it you shall surely die. (Genesis 2:15–17)

In verse 15, God tells Adam to "tend" the garden. How was Adam to carry this out—to tend a garden that is perfect? Perfect like it is in heaven. Simply put, to tend the garden meant that he was not to eat from the tree of the knowledge of good and evil. Under no circumstances was he to eat from the tree. God gave a simple, single-minded instruction to Adam.

Adam knew he would die if he ate of this tree. Even so, he decided to walk away from that single-minded instruction and transition into the realm of double-mindedness. He stopped letting God light his path, he went his own way, and he decided to make his own decisions. Simple enough.

We know how the story unfolded. The devil, representing himself as a serpent, came and tempted Eve. He suggested another direction separate from God's. The Enemy asked her, "Can it really be that God has said, You shall not eat from every tree of the garden?"

In response, she entertained the opportunity to deviate from what Adam had been told. The temptation to become double-minded. Did she see it like that? Probably not. None of us do. But it still led them away from God's wisdom. They now felt they had an option to go their own way. What Adam and Eve didn't realize was that there was no option, especially when it came to God's instructions. Complete obedience is required if we are going to stay single-minded.

Look at how the serpent speaks to them: "For God knows that in the day you eat of it your eyes will be opened, and you will be like God, knowing the difference between good and evil and blessing and calamity" (Genesis 3:5).

Our Father knows that we need His instruction to live and maintain a happy and peaceful life. We are literally on our own when we determine to go our own direction, left trying to cope with life and all its issues without divine help. That's too high a price. Adam and Eve didn't realize what damage was done by their decision. The innocent instruction that was given to them was now broken, and that cost them a close fellowship with the Father.

Being double-minded is always costly. When we break fellowship with the Father, we start fellowshipping with something else. The "something else" could be care, concern, or our human reasoning, or it could be circumstances thrown at us in this natural life.

Adam went from having a clear-cut mandate from God to becoming double-minded. Pretty simple. They did not tend to the garden as instructed. They broke that instruction and became aware of good and evil. They now had to discern between the two. God's created paradise was now gone.

This was the beginning of the natural world becoming double-minded. In reality, the double-mindedness probably started with Lucifer himself. Anytime we choose to go our own way, we are no different than the lost world. We become situational atheists, those who do not consult God.

Now look at verse 6: "And when the woman saw that the tree was good (suitable, pleasant) for food and that it was delightful to look at, *and a tree to be desired in order to make one wise*, she took of its fruit and ate; and she gave some to her husband, and he ate" (Genesis 3:6).

They were looking at the wisdom this tree offered. God wanted them to live in His wisdom, not to have to discern between good and evil. They were to simply let His infallible wisdom guide them and not struggle on their own. To live in *His House*. To let *Him* always be their *Home*.

Human reasoning was the world they had entered. Human reasoning occurs when a person breaks single-minded instructions from God to go their own way. We can blame the devil, or the serpent, but he did not force them to eat from the tree. He didn't force them to become double-minded. They chose to do that by taking his suggestion and following it over God's instruction. We are responsible for our decisions.

Verse 6 further states that they knew eating the fruit would make them wise. They were looking for self-sufficient wisdom, or wisdom outside God's wisdom. In today's world, it would be wanting more than or a different way than what is provided in the Bible. That sounds a lot like society today. It sounds a lot like Lucifer. Pride was found in his heart and he wanted to be like God (Ezekiel 28; Isaiah 14). I have to wonder if our desire to not follow God comes from the same source. The root of it is usually fear, pride, or wanting to sit on our own throne.

The rest of this story is well-known, sadly enough. Adam and Eve had to live with the decision they made. The divine favor they once enjoyed in their lives was severely hindered. They now had to struggle during childbirth and struggle with their children, and their life changed from one of God's amazing grace to one of works.

Why would we choose to not hear our heavenly Father daily? Not listening to Him is a poor choice. We have a Bible full of life-giving Scripture, but we opt to go our own way—not consulting godly counsel, not praying, and not coming to God. On top of it, we've been given Holy Spirit to lead and guide us. One of His jobs is to help us understand Scripture, so we really are without excuse.

DAVID AND GOLIATH

This story is one of the best examples of being single-minded in the Bible. Most people alive today have probably either heard the story or at least have a secular understanding of it. David didn't waver because of overwhelming circumstances when all the people around him had lost hope.

The nation of Israel was at war with their longstanding enemy and insurmountable foe, the Philistines (1 Samuel 17). I'll only touch a few high points, so feel free to read the entire story on your own.

The chapter begins, "Now the Philistines gathered together their armies for battle and were assembled at Socoh, which belongs to Judah, and encamped between Socoh and Azekah, in Ephes-dammim" (1 Samuel 17:1). Notice the words *which belongs to Judah*. Obviously, the enemy has trespassed into Israel's territory. In the ongoing battle between the Philistines and Israel for the territory, this was the standard operating procedure of the enemy.

The Enemy of our lives will always violate our territory with double-mindedness, sickness, disease, lack of finances, the feeling of overwhelm, tiredness, discouragement, self-promotion, greed, selfishness, etc. He will use whatever strategy is needed to neutralize us. The problem literally invades our lives uninvited. Remember, the Enemy's major goal is to violate our sense of well-being.

The Enemy also wants us to fall into drama (conflict). The minute we fall into drama, we have severely limited any chances of furthering the gospel. The drama will consume our lives. It's so deadly to the gospel that its sole reason for existing is to prevent anyone from being born again, filled with Holy Ghost, or healed. All of our time is consumed by ourselves or others who pull us into their messed-up world. We were commissioned to spread the gospel, not to be in contention with ourselves, others, or our circumstances.

Back to the story. These two nations were on opposing hillsides with a valley between them. For forty days, the Philistine champion Goliath stood in the valley and challenged Israel to send someone to fight him. Imagine every morning arising and hearing someone yelling slander and threats at you. That would get old fast, and maybe even bring fear. As well, Goliath stood nearly ten feet tall and had armor weighing one hundred and twenty-six pounds. His spearhead weighed over fifteen pounds alone.

Because of Goliath's sheer size and the intimidation that came with his size, he was dictating the rules of engagement with Israel. The Philistines had already trespassed into Judah's land. They were uncontrollable and creating havoc. The men of Israel weren't sure what to do. Fear had entered the camp and taken up residence in each one of them. They were truly double-minded. They had lost faith in the living God of Israel and were literally controlled by Goliath through the fear he brought.

Understand this: Our problems, and especially the Enemy, want to dictate the rules to us. How big is your giant problem that God can't help you overcome? Cancer says we have to die. Lack of money says we will go without. Meth dictates that our children will never fulfill their call on this earth. And to top it off, these forces introduce fear into our lives. Fear is the paralyzing factor. Fear is the opposite of faith and peace. We have to kill fear. Faith and peace are how we walk single-mindedly. Fear is how we continue in double-minded havoc. Havoc is defined as widespread destruction.

The soldiers in the army of Israel didn't want to fight a giant by themselves. These odds weren't fair. They knew it and Goliath knew it. It seemed there was no hope. And with the level of fear the army of Israel held, this was correct. But why was this the strategy of this particular battle? The Philistines, through Goliath, were dictating this battle. The army of Israel could have stormed the giant at any time and defeated him, but their fear blinded the soldiers from seeing that they were still part of an army.

Remember, Jesus, Holy Ghost, Father, and our brothers and sisters in Christ are our army. We are not alone. We have "a very present ... help in trouble" (Psalm 46:1). Isolation is a major tactic of the Enemy.

Goliath was taunting the men of Israel to come fight with him one on one. Isn't this how our problems speak to us? They can be intimidating. They can yell at us and say that we'll never beat them. We can't let that happen. We're to be moved and directed only by the Word of God. It's never ideal to let the circumstances dictate an outcome to us; that would be double-minded. Either we're going to honor God and stay single-minded to His instructions, or we're going to fall to the circumstances and become double-minded.

Goliath yelled out that if someone beat him, the whole Philistine nation would serve Israel. But if Goliath won, Israel would serve the Philistines. It didn't look good for Israel. They seemingly had no champions or any brave men to match Goliath. Fear was as much their giant as Goliath was: "When Saul and all Israel heard those words of the Philistine, *they were dismayed and greatly afraid*" (1 Samuel 17:11).

Dismayed in this verse means to be shattered, frightened, and terrified. *Greatly afraid* is the term for "to fear." When the problems in our lives attempt to take over, a resolve to follow God's instructions keeps us in a place of single-mindedness.

David entered the story at this point. The whole nation of Israel was shaking in their boots. They were so intimidated by the enemy that they couldn't hear and evaluate anything from God. When David came to the battlefield, he had a different perspective— an "all things are possible" perspective. God does the same with us. Oh, that we would let God come and invade our perspective. That we would let Him give us a fresh set of eyes through which to see our problems and lives. That we would let Him truly become Lord of our lives through single-mindedness and make us the overcomers He designed us to be.

David was on assignment from his earthly father, Jesse. He was bringing food to his three older brothers and the captain of the army. His assignment was to check on his brothers and let his father know how they were doing. As David was doing what his earthly father told him, Goliath stepped out of the enemy ranks and challenged the armies of Israel.

David reacted differently than the soldiers of Israel. He couldn't understand why no one would take Goliath's challenge. "Don't these men know that they serve the living God of all the earth?" he asked. David was single-minded and knew who his God was. He was not wavering because of Goliath's challenge. In fact, nowhere in this story does David even mention that Goliath is a giant. He calls him "an uncircumcised Philistine."

When David saw how the soldiers wavered at Goliath's threats, he couldn't fathom it. It should be unfathomable to us too. How can a problem dictate to us what the outcome should be? Why are we seeing a giant? We should be seeing a violation against God because it has come against us. "And David said to the men standing by him, What shall be done for the man who kills this Philistine and takes away the reproach from Israel? *For who is this uncircumcised Philistine that he should defy the armies of the living God?*" (1 Samuel 17:26).

It's time to see ourselves as God sees us. It is time to be single-minded to this truth.

Now let's step away from David's resolve to kill Goliath and look at verses 25 and 27: "And the Israelites said, Have you seen this man who has come out? Surely he has come out to defy Israel; the man who kills him the king will enrich with great riches and will give him his daughter and make his father's house free [from taxes and service] in Israel. ... And the [men] told him, Thus shall it be done for the man who kills him."

It is confirmed here to David, by the people, that whoever defeated Goliath would get King Saul's daughter, not have to pay taxes, and have lifelong financial security. It was a great incentive, but it had failed in motivating anyone into fighting Goliath. When we try to bribe God and attempt to fix our own problems by natural means, we will never solve anything spiritual. It's time to see these situations from a spiritual perspective.

David, I believe, was moved by the fact that Goliath was defying God by challenging Israel's army and *not* by the thought of winning the prize offered by King Saul. To David, this prize was only a benefit, a serendipity of defeating Goliath. David's main motivation was not his own benefit but God's honor. David was being single-minded in his devotion to both his earthly and heavenly father.

King Saul sent for David when he heard that he was asking about the reward for fighting Goliath. David, being a shepherd boy, was different from everyone else. He didn't seem afraid to fight the giant. Saul also noticed that the insolence of Goliath offended David. Saul observed a young man who possessed no fear. David had no fear because he was single-minded to the reason he wanted to fight.

David didn't have to debate or rethink things, which are the attributes of being double-minded. He was determined and full of resolve. It really made no sense to King Saul that David had no fear. Again, fear feeds double-minded thinking. There's no resolve when we aren't single-minded in our focus.

Saul tried to help David by putting him in his own personal armor. He assumed David would fight Goliath in the traditional manner—man to man, sword to sword, and shield to shield. But that wouldn't work and David knew it. The armor didn't fit. It wasn't God's solution to this problem. It may have appeared logical to wear armor to fight a giant, but it wasn't the answer for David and he knew it.

This was a form of religion, which is man's attempts at solving spiritual problems. David was true to himself, though. He didn't conform to the pressure around him—to man's solutions. The men around him had no answers. They had already succumbed to the pressure of Goliath and the Philistines. They were mentally defeated and had already lost the battle.

Wearing the armor would put him in the range of Goliath's death zone. The swing radius of Goliath's sword wouldn't have been a smart place for David to position himself. We can't fight the Enemy on his terms. We can't let circumstances dictate to us. No. We need the wisdom of God. The wisdom of God will fight the battle for us.

David tells King Saul that he isn't used to armor. He's never fought in it and today isn't the day to start. David also knew he wouldn't get a chance to engage Goliath if he faced him like that. David's decision to be authentic was what kept him safe. He could now operate in his true self.

His true self killed the lion and the bear. His true self fought without armor. David understood that he could stay away from the giant because he had a different weapon—one that wasn't like any other weapon on the battlefield that day. So David stayed far enough away from Goliath, thus stopping any chance of being struck by either sword or spear. He stayed in his place of safety.

Our place of safety is where we land when we listen to and follow the specific instructions given to us by our Father. To be authentic as David was, we need to obey. David understood he was on assignment, understood what weapon he was skilled with, and had an experience of winning in the past. David also knew who he was.

We must learn to do the same. Our place of safety is reached when we learn to rest in Father's instructions, stop looking at the circumstances in the natural realm, and see that following Father's instructions lets God fight for us. The battle is not ours but the Lord's (2 Chronicles 20:15). Our place of safety is reached when we fully realize that the promises in the Bible are more real than anything we face on this earth.

David's dialogue to King Saul was, "I have defeated the lion and the bear. They were attacking my father's sheep. If I defeated them, I will defeat this Philistine." He was telling Saul that the lion and bear were bigger feats than defeating Goliath. "I'll do what I do best. I operate in the unconventional. I'll do that again against this giant. My God will take care of this problem." Again, authenticity. Single-minded obedience comes when we become authentic to our true selves.

So, to be authentic, we have to first kill fear. Authenticity cannot thrive in fear. Learn to know God. Learn to sit at His feet. Let Him teach us. Let Him give us His faith. Know this: God's instructions, and/or a verse that we stand on in the Bible, will seem unconventional to the world, churches, and maybe our own methods of doing things. This is where real faith comes. Faith to stand on God's Word. His seed will change our situation. Our authenticity and His Word with obedience are unbeatable.

Now notice how David prepares to fight Goliath: "Then he took his staff in his hand and chose five smooth stones out of the brook and put them in his shepherd's [lunch] bag [a whole kid's skin slung from his shoulder], in his pouch, and his sling was in his hand, and he drew near the Philistine" (1 Samuel 17:40).

He went to the brook and chose five smooth stones. The brook was running with water. Water can be seen in Scripture as representing Holy Spirit. The Comforter. The One who will never leave us nor forsake us (Hebrews 13:5). He pulled "smooth, easy to fly at the enemy because there are no rough edges" stones. These stones represent the promises of God. They are Scripture verses that overcome our problems, a spoken *rhema* word for us. They are life given to us by Holy Spirit, and the solution to the problem. They are "the washing of water with the word" (Ephesians 5:26).

And why five stones? Because there are more Goliaths to come after this one is defeated. The Enemy of our soul and life will always bring another situation for us to solve. We'll need divine help with those issues as well. Goliaths aren't going away while we live on this earth. However, we win the battle because we have divine help and guidance. This is how we overcome. We are more than conquerors through Christ Jesus (Romans 8:37).

Notice what David now does after he secures his weapons and instructions from the Father:

Then said David to the Philistine, You come to me with a sword, a spear, and a javelin, but I come to you in the name of the Lord of hosts, the God of the ranks of Israel, Whom you have defied. This day the Lord will deliver you into my hand, I will smite you and cut off your head. And I will give the corpses of the army of the Philistines this day to the birds of the air and the wild beasts of the earth, that all the earth may know that there is a God in Israel. And all this assembly shall know that the Lord saves not with sword and spear; for the battle is the Lord's, and He will give you into our hands. When the Philistine came forward to meet David, David ran quickly toward the battle line to meet the Philistine. (1 Samuel 17:45–48)

David, in his unconventional approach to this battle scenario, has no doubt. In fact, he ran at Goliath—what had been a problem for Israel but not for him. Why? He had no fear. His fear was replaced by his faith in God. David knew there really wasn't a battle to be fought. All he had to do was land a stone in Goliath's forehead.

David was good at placing a stone wherever he slung it. This would be no different. There really was no battle. He was simply doing the cleanup work by making his brothers and the soldiers of Israel safe. Remember, his father Jesse asked him to go check on them.

David dictated the outcome to Goliath. He told him, "I will cut off your head. I will feed your body to the birds." In other words, Goliath could go back to the demons from whom he came. The stone from David's slingshot landed true, hitting Goliath in the forehead. I imagine as Goliath tumbled to the ground, shock and awe filled both camps. What was once an insurmountable problem had been handled in a few seconds— and by a youth. Sounds like God to me. He makes the "impossible" possible. And quickly.

David told Goliath he was going to cut his head off, but he had no sword. His slingshot wasn't equipped for that type of work. But then David took Goliath's sword out of his belt. He cut off Goliath's head with his *own* sword. Wow. God is not afraid of our enemies or how we view our inadequacies. Maybe it is time we see things as God does.

David decapitates Goliath and now has a trophy. All the men see that Jehovah is God. What the Enemy meant for evil, God turned to good (see Genesis 50:20). Cutting off the head was the proof of death back in that day. The death of a huge, looming enemy in this case.

But couldn't this be seen as the death of a major problem? When God's Word is acted upon by us, it will bring death to our problem. We can carry our "trophy" around as well. God's Word is proof of death to our problems.

Christ is the Head of the church. We are under his authority. Goliath, as seen in this story, represents the problems facing us. When we face problems, they are trying to impose their will over our lives. David said, "No!" and beheaded Goliath. Only God is the Head. Don't we do the same every time we listen to Holy Spirit's instructions? We're letting Christ be the Head of the church again. We're letting Him be our Head again. Remember, we have no other gods before Him (see Exodus 20:3).

"When the Philistines saw that their mighty champion was dead, they fled." Scripture tells us that the Israelites chased the Philistines all the way back to Gath (one of the five cities of the Philistine nation). We need to do exactly what the Israelites did in this story. We need to drive our problems back to where they came from. We need to drive them back from trespassing in our lives as these Philistines did with Israel. No longer will we let the Enemy impose his will on us. We have authority through Jesus' name, and the best way to know that authority is present in our lives is to obey the voice of our Father. To learn to follow the leadings of Holy Ghost, and be at rest in Him.

HALL OF FAITH

The Hall of Faith is the listing of faithful men and women in Hebrews 11. Let's take a look at some of these people.

Noah

[Prompted] by faith Noah, *being forewarned by God* concerning events of which as yet there was no visible sign, took heed and diligently and reverently constructed and prepared an ark for the deliverance of his own family. *By this [his faith which relied on God] he passed judgment and sentence on the world's unbelief* and became an heir and possessor of righteousness (that relation of being right into which God puts the person who has faith). (Hebrews 11:7)

This is so good. Noah honored God, stayed single-minded to what God told him, and look at the result: he became intimate with God. I'd rather be intimate with God than be intimate with my circumstances. Now look at the verse "By this [his faith which relied on God] he passed judgment and sentence on the world's unbelief." God's Word, His instructions, not only give us an answer but save us from the torment of the problem. Fear brings torment. But also notice this passage says he had faith in what God told him. The reason Noah is in the Hall of Faith is because he didn't waver when the odds were insurmountable.

Noah was a man of strong faith. He spent one hundred and twenty years building an ark and living in the ridicule that followed his decision to be obedient to God. He endured constant mockery from strangers, friends, and family. But Noah turned out to be correct in the end. He must have realized that he was right in the beginning as well. When it looked like he didn't have a trace of sanity, his sheer courage in obeying God made him correct. Noah's obedience saved all the animals inhabiting the earth, as well as his family. God was able to replenish the earth and start things in motion once again.

Moses

"[Urged on] by faith the people crossed the Red Sea as [though] on dry land, but when the Egyptians tried to do the same thing they were swallowed up [by the sea]" (Hebrews 11:29). This was an unconventional event. Of course, many such events were experienced by Israel during their release from Egypt. Every event was different in its own right, but all the events were from God. And while each one seemed uncomfortable for the nation of Israel, consider this: was finding the promised land worth it?

Getting out of slavery in Egypt was worth whatever price God asked and required. He was faithful to His word and He delivered. Moses accepted it all by faith. He stayed single-minded to God's instructions and led them out of Egypt. The children of Israel were double-minded and complained. Moses struggled at times, but his heart for God didn't.

The Israelites at Jericho

"Because of faith the walls of Jericho fell down after they had been encompassed for seven days [by the Israelites]" (Hebrews 11:30). Now for another unconventional story. Israel became single-minded to God's instructions, they obeyed them in detail, and in seven days Jericho was theirs. They didn't allow the tall walls to dictate the rules of engagement. They let God's word overcome the huge odds confronting them. With God, and us following His instructions, we are a majority.

They marched around Jericho for seven days. That's a long time without seeing results or understanding how their actions would make those mighty walls falter. I love how God's instructions often don't seem to make much sense at the time. God doesn't usually consult our limited belief system. That which is not of faith is sin. He is a faith being. That's all that moves Him.

Continue to read Hebrews 11 with this single-minded perspective. Remember, though, this is being single-minded to God's instructions. Look at how these heroes of faith didn't come up with their own solutions. They didn't listen to well-meaning friends. They followed God's Word concerning the solution to the problems facing them. And they did it like David did, before they even saw a solution in the natural. They believed God.

We have to come to the point in our walk with God that we

realize we can live this way too. God has put everything in us that we need to be faith beings. Holy Spirit is there, living inside us, and He is enforcing what was put in us. We are overcomers in this life. Losing is not an option. Hearing God and following Him is what divine living truly is. We have to come to this point in our lives, take ownership of this truth, and once and for all settle the issue.

It's time to stop wavering and being unstable. Instability comes when two opposing forces enter our thinking. It's time to kill one of those forces. The best way to do that is to follow Holy Spirit exclusively. Hear Him and listen to Him only. We will get this understanding if we continue to work at it and not give up.

Noah followed God's instructions for 120 years. We don't have to do that. Our perspective has to be one where we learn from our failures. Where we quit beating ourselves up and learn to get back up one more time. Where we learn to tell God we're ready for the next adventure. Where we not only tell God but show Him that we won't quit, and where we settle the issue and become single-minded to His purposes, His life, and His call for us.

Reading Scripture now, I see that every book from Genesis to Revelation contains a story of blessings from God through living single-minded versus living a defeated life through our own will in double-mindedness. Without exception this is a main truth all through the Bible.

GOOD VERSUS EVIL

An understanding of what *good versus evil* means will illuminate our walk with the Lord. If we don't understand something, we're not able to use it, much less let it operate in our lives. A lack of knowledge is one of the biggest problems in the body of Christ today.

The safest, most fulfilling place of abiding in God comes when we learn how to follow Him. We follow him by listening to His voice and/or honoring a portion of Scripture that solves our problem. This is how we get our direction. Following God exclusively is the ideal way to live. It's what Jesus did, and we are told we can do the same. Not many believe it. But walking single-mindedly is what brought true joy back to my life.

So, what is evil? Is it not staying away from sin? That does come into play. Is it a place of judgment? Does it come because of not honoring God? Some think so. I want us to understand that there are subtle decisions, which we do not give priority to each day, that are just as detrimental to our faith as the most blatant sin.

ADAM AND EVE

Let's consider Adam and Eve again. Eve obviously saw no real danger in eating the forbidden fruit. It didn't look dangerous. Like Eve, many of us believe we have a choice whether or not we are to pay attention to and do what the Father has told us. We march ahead and do what we think is best for us.

The Bible tells us to get wisdom and understanding from Scripture (2 Timothy 3:16–17), Holy Ghost (James 1:5), and our spiritual elders (Psalm 37:30). What in us makes us believe we don't really need all of God's benefits on a daily basis? Why is it that the only time we seem to ask for His help is when we encounter a problem? I really don't blame Eve much anymore. She did what many in the body of Christ do on a daily basis.

Father instructed Adam and Eve not to eat from the tree of the knowledge of good and evil—a very clear, direct instruction. Father only gives clear, direct, single-minded instructions. There will never be *any* deviation in how He instructs us. He doesn't second-guess Himself.

Adam and Eve didn't have an understanding of the ramifications of disobeying His instructions. If they did, they would have gained perspective to carry out God's instructions for them. The fact that they didn't listen to Him, and chose to go their own way instead, would change their lives forever. But not just theirs. Our lives are affected by their decision as well. We are in need of a Savior because of their actions.

Let's look at Genesis 3:5 again: "For God knows that in the day you eat of it your eyes will be opened, and you will be like God, *knowing the difference between good and evil and blessing and calamity.*" Reread the emphasized last portion. I believe Father wanted them in a world of blessings and not cursings. He wanted them in a world of life and not death. He wanted them to live in peace and harmony with Him, their Maker.

"And when the woman saw that the tree was good (suitable, pleasant) for food and that it was delightful to look at, and a tree to be desired in order *to make one wise,* she took of its fruit and ate; and she gave some also to her husband, and he ate" (Genesis 3:6). This verse is paramount, as it is the first place we see the decision between good versus evil presented. The tree, to Eve, looked suitable and pleasant. It appeared to her as an excellent choice—and it would make her wise. Hard to pass that one up.

Eve made a decision based on what she saw and what she was told by the serpent. It was a beautiful tree, good for food, and it would make her wise. What's not to like about that? And even though she'd been told not to eat of it, the tree appeared harmless. She must have thought, *It's okay. I don't see any reason not to eat it.*

Eve was being offered wisdom. The world we live in today is looking for wisdom too. We want to know how to succeed in our career, save money, make money, be cured of sickness, retire early, be happy, etc. And what's the most effective perceived way to do that? The natural world looks to wisdom. But the wisdom this tree was offering was the worldly kind, not God's wisdom that we truly desire. Scripture tells us to seek *His* wisdom.

Heavenly Father told Adam not to eat of this tree. His instruction had nothing to do with logic, with beauty, or with what anyone else was telling them. None of these things mattered. It was based on His divine wisdom that comes from His ability as the all-sufficient God that makes no error.

God knew what was best for them. He wanted them to stay innocent. To not have to decide. To not have to debate. To not have to suffer. He didn't want them to have to discern the difference between good and evil. Put simply, God didn't want Adam and Eve to have to deal with double-mindedness by eating of the tree. Living single-minded was His original design.

Why didn't they just follow His instructions? Why didn't they decide to stay innocent? We could say Eve didn't understand. We could say Adam didn't understand. Either way, it doesn't matter. The disobedience happened. They became double-minded and suffered the consequences. Actually, we all suffer the consequences of being double-minded as well. This is the reason our Father instructs us—to get us through the problem, to teach us His ways, and to lead us into life.

Let's look at the portion of Scripture that speaks of good versus evil. The King James Version says this: "For every one that useth milk is unskilful in the word of righteousness: for he is a babe. But strong meat belongeth to them that are of full age, even those who by reason of use have their senses exercised to discern both good and evil" (Hebrews 5:13).

Now here's the Amplified Bible Classic Edition:

For everyone who continues to feed on milk is obviously inexperienced *and* unskilled in the doctrine of righteousness (of conformity to the divine will in purpose, thought, and action), for he is a mere infant [not able to talk yet]! But solid food is for full-grown men, for those whose senses *and* mental faculties are trained by practice to discriminate *and* distinguish between what is morally good *and* noble and what is evil *and* contrary either to divine or human law.

An interesting portion of Scripture. As a pastor, I find that I've avoided it. I have an understanding of it, but it seemed too debatable in the church. (Just being honest. I want to be liked as much as the other guy.) But let's consider it now in light of what we've discovered from Adam and Eve's story.

Hebrews 5:14 in the AMPC states that "meat belongs to *full-grown men*." Mature people, in other words. Mature in the Word. Mature in listening, believing, and following God. Mature. This chapter further states that in this maturity one can discriminate and distinguish between what is good (what follows what the Father tells us and what is given to us in Scripture) and evil (what is contrary to divine or human law). Therefore, God's choice is obviously better than ours.

Mature people follow divine instructions. They follow what the Word of God instructs, not debating it or comparing it to what they think or what someone says. They simply follow that instruction. They know that God's instructions are the best way, and have come to the understanding that it no longer matters what they think. For them, the right judgment is what the Father tells them.

Eve debated the instructions given to them by God. Adam debated them as well. We all have debated in our thinking. Following what Holy Spirit tells us is not always the most convenient path to follow. Many times it won't be.

Think of the times you have been wronged by people. Scripture tells us to forgive others. Think of the times you had to make a hard decision. The "inner witness"—that part of you that hears God—gave you instructions. It didn't make sense. Most of the time it won't. But we trust our Father and do as He says. Mature people follow those instructions anyway. That's the beginning of learning to walk in the biblical wisdom spoken of here in Hebrews. If we don't follow, or if we continually choose to go our own way, we wouldn't be considered mature.

We are growing up in Him in all things (see Ephesians 4:15). He gives us a chance to learn. He isn't hard on us. He also gives us the wisdom spoken of in James 1:5: "If any of you lacks wisdom, let him ask of God" (NKJV). God's wisdom is to guide us and help us, to let us know we're not alone in the decision-making process. He is there to pull us through all trials, opportunities, and situations. And He does it with kindness.

Holy Spirit offers His assistance so we can learn to do the "meat" of His Word. With this assistance, we are able to follow His instructions over our desires, wants, and common sense. It makes us single-minded to His purposes.

The wisdom that Adam and Eve defaulted to, by their choice, was not God's wisdom. It was sensual, selfish, "so I can figure this out" wisdom—the world's wisdom. Father's original plan was to mature us and not have us needlessly struggle. Father wants us to follow Him, and do His will instead of our own, so we can finish the work He has for us on this earth.

True happiness comes in doing the Father's will. Not bouncing back and forth, trying to serve God and get the victory. Not trying to get help when we make another dumb mistake and we now need Him to pull us out of the fire. If we're living this way, going our own way, expressing our own opinion without considering the souls of other people, we are living on milk. We're acting like babies.

When we become mature, we have no issue laying our life down for Him. We also are then in a position to lay our life down for others. This is accomplished by following and obeying His instructions. Only by paying attention to what He tells us will we gain an understanding of how to lay our life down. Helping other people, fellowshipping, getting to know Him, and giving Him control over our lives is the way we are to live.

As the kingdom becomes our priority, things we want in this life will come to us as, Matthew 6:33 says: "Seek ye first the kingdom of God ... and all these things shall be added to you." We won't be left out of our hopes and dreams. He freely gives us all things (see Romans 8:32). This illuminates how our priorities line up with His. We are no longer mimicking the world, which is on a continual quest to get more for itself. Our focus is now on souls, saving the lost and being a person who shows His love. We care for more than just ourselves and our family. We are now about our Father's business as Jesus was. It has become our priority.

This may look like a sacrifice of our free will, but in reality it isn't. This is divine life. Paul called it our "reasonable service" (Romans 12:1 KJV). Giving to others is the place of freedom. Letting Holy Spirit lead us is the place of true life—the God-inspired life.

JESUS

Jesus always models the will of the Father. He always lays His will down for the instructions given to Him by Holy Spirit. He is our example to follow, and, in my opinion, He is the only example to follow.

In John 4 is the story of the woman at the well. This Samaritan woman had come to the well to gather water, and Jesus, being by Himself at the well, engaged her in conversation. It goes into much more detail than I'll address here, so feel free to read it on your own. I'm going to choose a few points to demonstrate Jesus's ability to follow His Father's instructions regardless of what others thought he should do. In other words, His singlemindedness.

Here's a bit of story background. Samaritans and Jews did not interact. The woman had come to the well at midday, which was not the customary time for drawing water in that culture. She had been married multiple times and was living with a man to whom she wasn't married. And most of all, Jews hated Samaritans. (Samaritans were half Jew and half Gentile because the Jews had intermarried with the Assyrians. They followed their own version of the first five books of the Bible and had their own form of worship.) Jesus crossed cultural and religious lines to follow the single-minded instructions of the Father.

The disciples, returning to Jesus after finding something to eat, discovered Him speaking with this woman. They would by no means talk with a Samaritan and were astonished that He was engaging her. So Jesus was obviously not following the custom of that day and honoring the Jewish rules about Samaritans. He did this a lot, by the way.

In the meanwhile his disciples prayed him, saying, Master, eat. But he said unto them, *I have meat to eat that ye know not of.* Therefore said the disciples one to another, Hath any man brought him ought to eat? Jesus saith unto them, *My meat is to do the will of him that sent me, and to finish his work.* (John 4:31–34 KJV)

Look at verse 34: "My meat is to do the will of Him that sent me, and to finish His work." Jesus was saying that He was following the instructions of His Father. He wasn't doing things the way He thought they should be done; He was following a higher calling and purpose, submitting His will to His Father's will.

His life was not His own. He connected with His Father and Holy Spirit (following the definition of maturity in Hebrews 5:13), and conformed to the *divine will* in purpose, thought, and action. He was discerning between double-minded milk and single-minded meat. He was discerning between good and evil. He was being single-minded.

So, considering chapter 3 of this book—the sower sowing the seed—Father planted a seed in Jesus. The seed was an instruction to engage the Samaritan woman. Jesus took that seed and was letting it grow—to full maturity. He was about His Father's business (see Luke 2:49).

Jesus's life was one of being good soil. Good soil is where seeds grow. His mind, will, and emotions yielded to the instructions given to Him. He knew why He came to earth: to save all those who were lost. He was making sure His soil was the best possible ground for harvest. He was modeling for us, and reaping 100 percent from the seed given to Him. None was wasted. None was lost. Jesus was the best soil, and the gardener of the seed the Father gave Him.

He was operating single-mindedly to the divine instructions delivered to Him. He wasn't looking at a Samaritan woman. He wasn't looking at the way she broke tradition. He wasn't looking at the fact that she was living with a man. In fact, He connected with her in such a way that she was the one who delivered His message to her village—who brought salvation to her people. She was touched by Him and wanted everyone to experience the miracle that was Jesus.

In two days, the entire village of the Samaritan woman had the gospel preached to them. Jesus was able to "save" people who hadn't heard and were lost, because He followed the instructions delivered to Him by Father. He ministered to a lowly, despised Samaritan woman, and this conversation led to this village having the gospel preached to them. Father's instructions always carry a higher purpose than our methods. Learning to follow Him is a much better way to live.

Remember the parable of the sower: the soil, the seed, the birds, and hearing. With that in mind, Jesus took the seed (the instruction of Father) and planted it in His heart. He protected it from all opinions, adversarial input, and even well-meaning friends. Jesus protected His ability to hear His Father over anything else, and then walked it out with single-minded resolve. Not wavering. Not second-guessing. Following those instructions even to the cross.

This is how Jesus walked without sin. This is how He was fully mature, and how He discerned good versus evil. He knew *good* was following the will of the Father, and *evil* was going His own way. He modeled it for us so we could walk in it as well. And if He modeled it, we can too.

JESUS MODELS FOR US

One of the most wonderful portions of Scripture is Mark 4:35–41. The same story is recounted in Luke 8:22–25, and both accounts provide thought-provoking aspects of how the kingdom of God operates. Jesus models for us how to listen to Father.

On that same day [when] evening had come, He said to them, Let us go over to the other side [of the lake]. And leaving the throng, they took Him with them, [just] as He was, in the boat [in which He was sitting]. And other boats were with Him. And a furious storm of wind [of hurricane proportions] arose, and the waves kept beating into the boat, so that it was already becoming filled. But He [Himself] was in the stern [of the boat], asleep on the [leather] cushion; and they awoke Him and said to Him, Master, do You not care that we are perishing? And He arose and rebuked the wind and said to the sea, Hush now! Be still (muzzled)! And the wind ceased (sank to rest as if exhausted by its beating) and there was [immediately] a great calm (a perfect peacefulness). He said to them, Why are you so timid *and* fearful? How is it that you have no faith (no firmly relying trust)? And they were filled with great awe *and* feared exceedingly and said one to another, Who then is this, that even wind and the sea obey Him?

Notice in verse 35 that Jesus gives the disciples an instruction: "Let us go over to the other side." This is a seed. Jesus had just finished teaching the parable of the sower. Now He was going to let them experience a "working model" of what he just shared.

Jesus was telling them what they needed to do: cross over to the other side of the lake. He wanted to accomplish something. Jesus didn't go into detail as to why they were crossing over. He simply informed them that they were going.

Many times when Holy Spirit informs and instructs us, He doesn't give all the details. We don't always know why we're doing what He has told us to do. This is where faith in the word spoken comes in—the faith we see demonstrated by the "heroes of faith" found in Hebrews 11. God didn't give them all their instructions up-front.

Often, we want to figure out what God is doing. Sometimes we even put our spin on it. But if we knew exactly how to do it, wouldn't we be seeing from our own knowledge? Eve was told she would be wise if she ate of the tree. She would be able to figure it out and would then be able to discern on her own. Humans are always wanting out of a problem, wanting more for themselves, trying to find a way for more comfort, or simply trying to figure it out.

Back to Mark 4. Jesus's instructions contained no details concerning their trip. He was simply telling the disciples what to do. Jesus had total reliance on what His Father instructed. He was following the lead of Holy Spirit. In fact, Jesus was resting—literally asleep in the back of the boat—because He was doing what was instructed. Faith should be a place of rest, not a place of striving. Striving isn't rest. Striving would indicate a place of not believing, a place of double-mindedness.

Think of it this way: when we are instructed by Holy Spirit

and choose to follow His instructions, we rest. If our soil is good soil, the crop will come up. If we have strife or concern, we may be thorny or rocky soil. The seed (instruction) given to us is struggling to grow in that kind of soil. In good soil, there is less struggle.

Good soil is a heart yielded to the leadings and instructions of our Father. A rocky or thorny soil (heart or mindset) will make the plant strive to grow. It will be difficult to carry out the instructions Holy Spirit has given us because we are striving to know. We are striving to understand. We are not at rest.

Take a look at James 1:2–4: "Consider it a sheer gift, friends, when tests and challenges come at you from all sides. You know that under pressure, your faith life is forced into the open and shows its true colors. So don't try to get out of anything prematurely. Let it do its work so you become mature and well-developed, not deficient in any way" (MSG). This passage of Scripture clearly shows how Jesus walked. He was not deficient in any way concerning his faith life. Thus, he was asleep in the back of the boat as they crossed the lake. He did what he was instructed; to do so he was resting, not striving.

Jesus is our model for this life. He is our example. We too are able to rest after we have received divine instructions, regardless of how the outcome of our situation looks. This is true faith. It is single-mindedness, and it is the path to the greater works.

Mark 4:36–37 speaks of a violent storm on the lake. The Greek word used indicates it was a hurricane-force storm. We could say it was a worst-case scenario. And yet, the instructions given to Jesus were more of a reality in his life than a hurricane. Later in His life, the instructions given to Jesus would be more real than the suffering and shame of going to a cross to die for us.

Walking single-mindedly is not always convenient. It makes God and His instructions first in our lives. Our desires and fears have to take a backseat. It's a learned process. We get there as we practice listening and then obeying.

The disciples, in the same passage, had been fighting the storm in their own strength and wisdom. They were experienced fishermen and had been in plenty of storms. They understood the water and knew how to navigate in any condition. But this storm was more intense. The boat was full of water and they feared they would die.

The disciples obviously were "going to the other side" in their own strength. They understood what was said, but they defaulted to the way it was always done—the way they were trained. They were accessing the fruit in the garden promised to Eve that would make them wise (human wisdom). It wasn't the way Jesus was training them.

In verse 38 Jesus was awakened by the disciples, who were in complete distress. Distress will always try to disrupt our faith, and will always try to disrupt God's instructions for us. Distress is designed to alter the course of instructions delivered to us by Holy Spirit. But that distress didn't affect Jesus. He stood up and said to the hurricane, "Peace, be still." The storm went from hurricane-force winds to total peace. Talk about changing the circumstances.

What was the difference? The disciples had the same tools as Jesus. They had the same instructions as Jesus. The answer comes in John 4:40: "Why are you so timid and fearful? How is it that you have no faith (no firmly relying trust)?" *No faith*. Jesus was saying to the disciples, "You were able to stop this and you didn't." They had the tools but didn't use them—but why? Why did they so quickly forget the Master's instructions when a problem arose?

Anytime we default to human reasoning or what we can see in the natural realm, we are out of faith. We've left the instructions given to us by Holy Spirit. The disciples may have honored Jesus's instructions, but what happened when the storm came? What happened to their resolve to follow Him when things became unfavorable?

Jesus was telling them, "You lost faith in the words I gave

you, which were 'let us go to the other side.'" The disciples
looked at the circumstances, the hurricane-force storm, and
their focus changed from following what Jesus said, to fighting
the storm. Jesus gave them His word, and it was enough to overcome all obstacles. His word was enough to get them to the
other side.

Likewise, His words are enough for us to overcome our
storms. They are enough. They are life. Oh, that we would learn
to honor His words. When we honor His words, He fights for
us. He defeats the storm for us.

If we are walking out God's will, He will get us to the other
side—whatever that other side may be. This has to go from a
Bible story to a reality in our lives. We can no longer say, "Oh,
that was Jesus. He was the Son of God, so He was different."
Does Scripture not say "as He is, so are we in this world" (1 John
4:17)? If we are followers of Christ—and we are—then we have to
get this. We have to know what it means to have faith. Or, in our
times of struggle, how are we to get continued help?

Not only did the disciples have a word from Jesus, but He
also was in the boat with them. At any point on the journey
across the lake, they were able to wake Jesus and get instructions
about the storm. Look at James 1:5–8:

If you don't know what you're doing, pray to the Father. He
loves to help. You'll get his help, and won't be condescended to
when you ask for it. Ask boldly, believingly, without a second
thought. People who "worry their prayers" are like wind-
whipped waves. Don't think you're going to get anything from
the Master that way, adrift at sea, keeping all your options open
(MSG).

Jesus was never overcome by circumstances. Jesus was the
disciples' wisdom. They saw Him live His faith without fail.
James 1 says that if anyone lacks wisdom (understanding), let him
ask of God who freely gives. It even says we will not be scolded
in the process. At any time on the journey we can get the help

we need. Holy Spirit will never leave us nor forsake us (see Deuteronomy 31:6).

Holy Spirit will tell us what to do. As many times as we need to hear His instruction, He gives it. He has no issue repeating the instructions until we get it. This is what James 1:2–8 is saying.

JONAH

The book of Jonah is an intriguing story. Many of us have heard this one since childhood, but there's more to it than Jonah getting swallowed by a big fish. This story is an account of both single- and double-mindedness.

Jonah was given specific instructions from God: "Go to Nineveh and proclaim against it." The Ninevites were going to be destroyed unless they repented. This wasn't hard for Jonah to interpret, but he decided to go his own way—to be double-minded.

Let's break it down verse by verse starting with the first chapter. "Arise, go to Nineveh, that great city, and proclaim against it, for their wickedness has come up before Me" (Jonah 1:2). This is a straightforward instruction. Jonah can't deny this one. God wanted to save this lost nation, and He uses people to accomplish His plans on the earth—in this case, Jonah.

But Jonah rose up to flee to Tarshish from being in the presence of the Lord [as His prophet] and went down to Joppa and found a ship going to Tarshish [the most remote of the Phoenician trading places then known]. So he paid the appointed fare and went down into the ship to go with them to Tarshish from being in the presence of the Lord [as His servant and minister]. (Jonah 1:3)

Obviously, Jonah didn't want to do as God told him. He had no care nor concern for Nineveh. The reality is that the Hebrews hated the Ninevites. Jonah was no different, and he chose to become double-minded to God's instructions. He did an interesting thing, though: he became single-minded in his rebellion by running from God. He knew if he went and did as God has instructed, God would save Nineveh. He didn't want this to happen, so he picked the most remote trade route and location possible, Tarshish. He was literally on the run. He went to Tarshish to run "from being in the presence of the Lord."

How do you run from the Lord? You don't. It's not possible. Now look at verse 4: "But the Lord sent out a great wind upon the sea, and there was a violent tempest on the sea so that the ship was about to be broken."

It is never a wise decision to run from God. There are storms of rebellion that we bring upon ourselves, and this was what was happening here. This storm, however, was different from the one Jesus encountered in the last chapter. Jesus's storm in Mark 4 was brought on by the enemy of our soul to stop the work of the gospel. Jonah's storm was a self-imposed, disobedient mess.

When storms come, the thing that saves us is our obedience. In disobedience, we don't have that assurance. We are usually in His grace—or mercy. And yes, He comes and rescues us when we call upon Him. He is our Father, after all. I love Him for that. Now see how the mariners are affected by Jonah's disobedience.

"Then the mariners were afraid, and each man cried to his god, and they cast the goods that were in the ship into the sea to lighten it for them. But Jonah had gone down into the inner part of the ship and had lain down and was fast asleep" (Jonah 1:5). Jonah's behavior wasn't a normal response to a life-threatening storm. He was asleep. Did justifying his decision to rebel against God allow him to sleep during an obvious crisis? This was a single-minded decision to not serve God.

Everyone else was terrified of this storm, so why wasn't Jonah? Look at verse 6:

"So the captain came and said to him, What do you mean, you sleeper? Arise, call upon your God! Perhaps your God will give a thought to us so that we shall not perish." Jonah wasn't going to get clarification from God here. He wanted no clarification. He knew why the storm was raging—because he was double-minded to God's instructions.

This storm was on Jonah. It was a storm of rebellion—a "not obeying God" storm. It makes me wonder about the cause of some of our storms. I always ask people who are facing a big obstacle, "What has Holy Spirit told you to do?" Most who are in a huge struggle tell me the same thing: "I don't know." Or worse, "I haven't asked Him."

Now let's look at verses 7–8:

And they each said to one another, Come, let us cast lots, that we may know on whose account this evil has come upon us. So they cast lots and the lot fell on Jonah. Then they said to him, Tell us, we pray you, on whose account has this evil come upon us? What is your occupation? Where did you come from? And what is your country and nationality?

Jonah was the culprit. The passengers on the boat were trying to figure out why he was running. Why was he not honoring his God? Even they understood the power of obedience. Jonah's disobedient attitude put everyone on the ship in peril of losing their life. Our actions—obedient or disobedient—affect other people besides ourselves. That's why we need to seriously consider what God is doing in our life.

Picking the story up again in verse 9: "And he said to them, I am a Hebrew, and I [reverently] fear *and* worship the Lord, the God of heaven, Who made the sea and the dry land." Jonah's behavior didn't line up with this statement. Up to this point, he was cavalier, not considering the implications of following God's instructions. Now he finally realized that his rebellion had also affected the other people in the boat. He put *everyone* in peril.

His statement that he reverently worships the Lord makes me think he wanted life on his own terms. That will never happen. Jonah is not God (and neither are we). When we run from God and His instructions, aren't we doing the same? That which is not of faith is sin.

Now look at verse 10: "Then the men were exceedingly afraid and said to him, What is this that you have done? For the men knew that he fled from being in the presence of the Lord [as His prophet and servant], because he had told them." These men were amazed that Jonah would so blatantly disobey God. Even as heathens, they had more respect for their gods. They were now in fear because their lives were in jeopardy. Jonah's decision affected them. Selfishness is a double-minded action that disregards the instructions of God.

Then they said to him, What shall we do to you, that the sea may subside *and* be calm for us? For the sea became more and more [violently] tempestuous. And [Jonah] said to them, Take me up and cast me into the sea; so shall the sea become calm for you, for I know that it is because of me that this great tempest has come upon you. (vv. 11–12)

The storm continued to rage and worsen. Jonah admitted that he was the problem. His disobedience was the issue. His solution: "Throw me over."

This was an interesting choice. He surrendered to the circumstances, admitting that he could go no farther. His plans to run were not going to pan out. He had put too many people in jeopardy.

Likewise, our plans sometimes don't always go as expected and we struggle. We don't know why. Perhaps Jonah's example of disobedience sheds some light on that. In the areas we are struggling, we should go back to the last thing Holy Spirit said to us. We can start there to see if we can get clarification on the storm we are facing. Remember, we can always ask for clarification again. When we get it and rest, then He can fight the storm for us.

Nevertheless, the men rowed hard to bring the ship to the land, but they could not, for the sea became more and more violent against them. Therefore they cried to the Lord, We beseech You, O Lord, we beseech You, let us not perish for this man's life, and lay not upon us innocent blood; for You, O Lord, have done as it pleased You. (vv. 13–14)

The empathy of these sailors is admirable. Even as heathens, they obeyed Jonah's God more than Jonah did. They saw the power of God. Look at verse 14 in *THE MESSAGE*: "Then they prayed to God, 'O God! Don't let us drown because of this man's life, and don't blame us for his death. You are God. Do what you think is best.'"

These men now knew who Jonah's God was. They needed no convincing of that fact. They had respect and a newfound honor for Jonah's God. Jonah's dishonor of his own God was demonstrated by his level of double-minded disobedience. These men were aware that Jonah's God has the power of life and death. They also saw that Jonah's God is the Creator of the land and sea. So what was the solution for a double-minded disobedient person who does not honor his God?

"So they took up Jonah and cast him into the sea, and the sea ceased from its raging. Then the men [reverently and worshipfully] feared the Lord exceedingly, and they offered a sacrifice to the Lord and made vows" (v. 15). What comes to mind from this portion of Scripture is that it's better to obey than to sacrifice (1 Samuel 15:22). These sailors had experienced a fantastic event: the storm stopping. They now experienced the fear of the Lord. They were reverent and thankful to Jehovah, and they offered a sacrifice to Jonah's God and made vows. While Jonah had been disobedient and cavalier to Jehovah, these men had reverence because they'd experienced the God who delivered them. Amazing.

"Now the Lord had prepared and appointed a great fish to swallow up Jonah. And Jonah was in the belly of the fish three days and three nights" (v. 17). Ouch. Three days and nights in a big fish's belly. I think we'd all agree that it's better to obey God than to vacation in stomach acid.

Jonah now had a lot to consider. He was heading back to Nineveh, and not in the form or fashion he would have preferred. The three days in the fish's belly gave him plenty of time to think, repent, and make a decision to be obedient to the instructions of God.

When the fish spit Jonah up on the beach, something interesting happened. God asked him again if he would go to Nineveh and tell the city to repent. This time Jonah had enough sense to obey, and God gave him another chance. I love the mercy and kindness of our Father. He will give us another chance if we'll just simply humble ourselves and ask Him.

The city of Nineveh took three days to cross. It was a large, premier city in the region. Even from the first day, Jonah began preaching that the city of Nineveh would be demolished in forty days. The Ninevites heeded Jonah's warning and turned from their evil ways. From the king down to the lowest person, all the citizens repented. All fasted and put on sackcloth, even the animals. It was the revival of an entire city—a miracle of epic proportions. The entire city was saved because of their single-minded focus to follow God. They believed God more than Jonah did.

The eye-opener is that obeying God and staying single-minded to His divine instructions is the way of safety. It is truly the easiest way to live our lives. We need to ask ourselves if the storm we're in is one of resistance from the Enemy because we are in God's will for our life, or if the storm we're in is one of not being obedient to His instructions. Either way, our Father and Holy Spirit will come and rescue us.

What's the difference between Jesus going to the other side and Jonah running from instructions? Let's look at that in more detail.

COMPARING JONAH TO JESUS

In Jonah 1, Jonah got on a boat and ran from God because of his disobedience. In Mark 4, Jesus got on a boat and followed instructions from God because of His obedience.

Two men on different boats encountered a storm. Jonah's storm was as bad as the storm Jesus faced, with hurricane-force winds. Both boats and crews were in distress. Both were about to sink, and all aboard would perish. Natural answers and options no longer helped in these dire, life-ending situations.

Jonah was awakened by distraught sailors. They wanted him to pray to his God. Maybe Jonah's God could tell them why they were sinking.

Jesus was awakened by his distraught disciples. They were looking for an answer to their problem by asking Jesus for help, although they did sound a bit accusatory when they asked, "Don't you care that we perish?" Sometimes when we're in a storm and need an immediate escape, we can become very accusatory.

Both Jonah and Jesus were awakened to provide an answer to a problem. Jonah's answer would reveal to his crew why they were in distress: his disobedience. The death they were about to experience was totally Jonah's fault. Jesus's answer would bring a solution to the problem they were facing. Jonah was the problem while Jesus was the solution.

Jesus spoke to His storm and there was a great calm. Peace came over the sea. Total peace. What was on the inside of Jesus now manifested to the external circumstances. Obedience. On the other hand, Jonah had no such result. What was on the inside of Jonah was exactly what was on the outside of him: a storm. Disobedience. The outside world could not—and cannot —be made to conform to God's will through double-mindedness on our part.

Jesus's boat sailed in calm waters to the other side. Jonah had no such luck. As he was thrown over into the raging sea, a peace came on the sea. But Jonah was not saved by a boat ride or obedience. He was transported in a fish's belly from his place of disobedience, no longer the master of his situation. The attitude of being in charge and running from God was superseded by gross circumstances—being in the digestive system of a fish. Jesus operates in grace. Jonah was saved by mercy. Even though the stories are similar, they didn't yield the same result for either boat or man.

When He arrived on land, Jesus set a man free of total demonic possession. This man was so possessed he had to be chained. When the Gadarenes, who dealt with him, saw this demoniac in his right mind, fear came upon them and they begged Jesus to leave. They weren't sure how to accept this miracle.

Because of the fear, Jesus left the demoniac behind. He realized that the demoniac's testimony and newfound faith were enough to change this region. The demoniac, now turned evangelist, became single-minded to that task. The country knew this man and his story. They didn't know Jesus and weren't going to give any heed to Him. The demoniac's single-minded instructions from Jesus were to save his country. He was to tell his story of how he was lost but now was found. He once was bound, but now was free. To continue in that freedom, he chose to follow Jesus's instructions.

Jonah encountered receptive circumstances when he landed in Nineveh. He preached to the country of God's impending judgment, and the Ninevites repented and came to God. The whole incident with the storm and the fish swallowing Jonah swayed him from his selfish disobedience to finally serving God. Since he realized that he had no authority to calm the storm, he repented while in the fish's belly. His double-mindedness to not do God's will was costly, not only for Jonah but for the innocent sailors on the ship who almost lost their lives.

Jesus is single-minded to the Father's will. He is equipped because He is perfectly aligned with heaven. Jesus has all authority to remedy problems because He is on divine assignment. His soul is submitted to His spirit. Our spirit wants to follow God. Our submitted, renewed soul will join in with our spirit and follow God's instructions. Jesus was the master at this.

Jonah was not aligned with anything but his own selfish desires. Even though he had tremendous results with the entire nation of Nineveh being saved, he still was not happy. He wanted them to be destroyed. Jonah went back to being double-minded and returned to his prejudice against the Ninevites.

Jesus's only desire was to do the will of the Father. He realized He would be rejected by the people as He went to the land of the Gadarenes. Jesus, unlike Jonah, only got one redeemed—the demoniac. Just one. Not the whole country as Jonah did.

Our perspective has to be one of following our Father. The results, in the natural realm, will most likely oscillate. The eternal God does not oscillate. He is fixed and stable. As Jesus followed God, He had fixed and stable results. Jesus considered His Father's instructions more relevant. The victory is in following our Father. If we could only learn to walk by faith and not by sight (see 2 Corinthians 5:7).

What is the moral of these two stories? One man obeys and has results that are small in man's eyes, while the other is disobedient and yet has amazing results. Maybe being single-minded has little to do with results and more to do with listening to divine instruction. God knows the real solution and what the needs are. We go by perceived needs most of the time—what we want and consider to be a success. My prayer is that we get a heavenly perspective.

The Father is wanting to save this world and bring it back to His love and goodness. He is about souls and winning the lost. Saving those who need to be off drugs. Stopping the abuse happening to innocent people. This is why Jesus said, "Not My will but Yours, Father" (see Luke 22:42).

Jesus told us, "As Jonah was three days and three nights in the belly of the great fish, so will the Son of Man spend three days and three nights in the heart of the earth" (Matthew 12:40 NKJV). He was speaking of going to hell so we don't have to. Could the three days in hell be the price paid for us—so we could do His single-minded instructions? Perhaps not only salvation, healing, deliverance, and prosperity, but also the ability to be obedient and follow Holy Spirit? I think so. Jesus always modeled for us. He paid the price for us so we could do as He did.

Look at this Scripture. Notice the bolded words. Jesus modeled so we could do it as well. This should now shed more light on this truth: "**He**rein **is** our love made perfect, that **we** may have boldness in the day of judgment: because **as he is**, **so are we** in this world" (1 John 4:17 KJV).

On the other hand, Jonah was mad at God. He knew that God would save Nineveh, and he was so angry he asked God to take his life. God said He would not. Jonah threw a fit—lying in the sun outside the city, angry for not getting his way. Crazy drama-queen behavior. He still hated the fact that God proved His character and saved 120,000 people. He wanted them destroyed. He was still not lined up with God's vision.

Even so, God used Jonah's obedience even though Jonah truly felt contrary in his heart. Imagine what could have occurred if Jonah had the same heart to please his Father as Jesus did. What mighty exploits could have been achieved.

The reason some do exploits is they catch God's heart and desires. They have surrendered to His will. They don't consider it a high price to follow Him. It goes from "paying a price" to becoming an honor. In that honor to serve Him is where the real peace resides in our lives. He has redeemed us and made us whole. The least we can do is let Him have the ascendency in our lives.

As we learn to walk in the ways of our Father, we will learn to know Him on a much more intimate level. This "knowing Him more" is the key to not defaulting to the adversity we will have in our lives. We are not getting out of the storms and decisions required in this lifetime. Our Father desires to walk with us through all life throws at us. He wants us to learn to walk with Him the way He does. He wants us to have His heart and desires for the people we encounter day after day. If we choose, He wants us to have exploits. He just doesn't want to be left out of those exploits.

JEHOSHAPHAT

Jehoshaphat's story is an interesting study in being both single-minded and double-minded. He models both choices in detail, showing the results of being single-minded and prospering but also experiencing double-minded moments and struggling in life. His story is found in 2 Chronicles 17–21.

When Jehoshaphat had a single-minded focus to obey God, Judah prospered, was safe, and was a strong nation. He was truly committed to serving God. Deep down he had a heart for God, especially at the beginning of his reign as king.

Jehoshaphat began his reign when he was thirty-five years old, and he ruled for twenty-five years, dying at the age of sixty. He sent priests throughout the nation to teach the people the ways of God, and tore down the shrines and sex shops of the day. Look at how *THE MESSAGE* describes it in 2 Chronicles 17:6: "He was single-minded in following God, and he got rid of the local sex-and-religion shrines." That is epic! He was a godly king.

The kingdoms that surrounded Judah would bring him gifts, silver, and livestock. They wanted to stay in his good graces. The Philistines, especially, didn't want to ever wage war with him. He was to be feared because God was with him and everyone knew it. He had an army of one million and sixty thousand men. No one wanted to engage in war with Judah.

But the day came when wicked King Ahab of Israel wanted to create an alliance with him. What Ahab truly wanted was Jehoshaphat's support so that the huge army of Judah could make war on a neighboring kingdom, Ramoth-Gilead. This presented a double-minded decision for Jehoshaphat, and he began deviating from his instructions by aligning with King Ahab. A double-minded decision is usually not about doing what Holy Spirit wants. When we consider that there are options other than what Father has told us, we have the potential of becoming double-minded. To model Jesus, we can never consider the Father's word an option. God, who is not double-minded, is the safest place for us to abide. Always, without question.

I have to wonder if Ahab's deception and greed came from his time living with Jezebel. He was inherently selfish to his own desires, but Jezebel did have an effect on him too, and she was known for hating the prophets and the ways of God. She was also about control and having things her way.

Jehoshaphat wanted to consult with the prophets before he took part in the attack on Ramoth-Gilead. He was trying to hear from God for instructions. It was really a bit too late for this since Jehoshaphat was pleasing Ahab more than honoring God. He had to feel that something wasn't right and know that he was in disobedience already. He was trying to justify his actions. Not a good place to live. Obedience is better than justifying rebellion.

Ahab stated that his four hundred prophets approved of the plan. However, there was one prophet, Micaiah, who did not approve. In fact, this prophet boldly told Ahab that he person-ally would not return from the war. He further stated that if Ahab did not die in the war, that he, Micaiah, was not a prophet. That was a bold proclamation.

Neither Jehoshaphat nor Ahab heeded this prophet. The other four hundred prophets were afraid for their lives, so they prophesied what Ahab wanted to hear. Jehoshaphat heard from the Lord through what Micaiah spoke to them: he was as guilty as Ahab for disobedience to the prophetic word. Micaiah suffered dearly at Ahab's hand because he spoke the truth and did not waver.

When they engaged in war with Ramoth-Gilead, the results were dismal. Ahab asked Jehoshaphat to dress up in royal robes, and Jehoshaphat was placed in Ahab's chariot instead of Ahab. Was he trying to make sure Jehoshaphat died? This was no friend. This was no alliance. The guy was a rat. Why was Jehoshaphat going along with such a scheme?

Ahab knew they had a bounty on his own head. He didn't care about Jehoshaphat. He only cared about himself, his lust, and his desires. And Ahab, the coward that he was, dressed up like a regular soldier and mixed with the troops. He must have felt safe there. Was he thinking he would take over Jehoshaphat's huge army and get Ramoth-Gilead to boot?

Jehoshaphat was chased down by enemy soldiers who thought he was Ahab. When they realized he wasn't, they stopped the pursuit of him and left him alone. Talk about the favor of God. Ahab, hiding in with the troops, suffered a traumatic outcome. An enemy soldier threw a spear randomly into the ranks of soldiers and hit Ahab with it. He was struck between the lower armor and the breastplate—a wound proved to be fatal. Ahab died later that day.

God still honored Jehoshaphat even though he was in a precarious situation. Jehoshaphat had his grandfather David's "heart towards God." There is much God will do for us when we have a heart for Him. Our head may be wrong, and we may be disobedient to His instructions, but He will walk with someone who truly wants to serve Him. This is called grace (whereas what God extended to Jonah in his blatant stupidity and rebellion is called mercy). Thank God for His glorious grace toward us.

Jehoshaphat's life was spared even though he was betrayed by

Ahab. His life was spared even though he disregarded Micaiah, and was disobedient to God. A lesson learned for Jehoshaphat.

He came home from the war and instituted laws to turn the people back to God. He was careful about how his people were judged, ensuring everyone was treated fairly and the principles of God were always observed. He was single-minded toward Jehovah again, back in a place of safety.

In 2 Chronicles 20, more trouble was brewing: "Some time later the Moabites and Ammonites, accompanied by Meunites, joined forces to make war on Jehoshaphat. Jehoshaphat received this intelligence report: 'A huge force is on its way from beyond the Dead Sea to fight you. There's no time to waste—they're already at Hazazon Tamar, the oasis of En Gedi'" (vv. 1–2 MSG).

What does Jehoshaphat do? "Shaken, Jehoshaphat prayed. He went to God for help and ordered a nationwide fast. The country of Judah united in seeking God's help—they came from all the cities of Judah to pray to God" (vv. 3–4).

Jehoshaphat became single-minded again. He went and heard from God. Prayer and fasting is a great aid in curbing double-mindedness. If we are struggling to hear, this is our answer. Pray and fast. That was what Jehoshaphat had the entire kingdom of Judah do.

In the last chapter in this book, all of Nineveh prayed and fasted. They were spared. Don't miss this point. It's when we come back to God with a repentant heart that things change for us. God walks with someone who has a repentant heart.

Jehoshaphat had the nation of Judah do the same thing. Everyone from the greatest to the least was attentive and listening to God. The prophets told Judah that the war would be won, and great rejoicing broke out all over the kingdom. They heard that the battle was the Lord's and not the people's. I love how God took care of them. I love how God will take care of us as well.

The people were encouraged and there was a celebration in Judah. Jehoshaphat had a choir, in holy robes, march in front of his army as they went out to battle. Think about this move: Worship in the midst of a battle. Worship in the midst of a trial. That is what Judah was doing. They were worshipping.

Were they going to fight? They were making plans to do that, but they discovered that worship was the answer in the middle of this war. Since the battle was the Lord's, they were rejoicing and singing a song of praise. They moved to a place of worship. We must learn to live in a place of worship too. Don't fellowship with fear, doubt, and anger. Instead, learn to fellowship with Holy Spirit. "Those who worship Him must worship Him in Spirit and truth" (John 4:24).

As they marched forward to engage the enemy in battle, they came upon a most-interesting situation: the enemy was dead. The opposing armies had become confused and turned on each other. The battle was the Lord's. He told the nation of Judah and King Jehoshaphat that He would fight the battle for them. Judah didn't even have to fight.

They sought God, listened to His instructions, and worshipped Him. Through this, they turned their hearts back to the Lord, and He delivered the victory for them. God, in His infinite mercy, saved the entire nation of Judah. All they had to do was go out and gather the spoils. Talk about the grace of God coming through in an overwhelming situation.

Jehoshaphat and the people had a parade and celebrated. Everybody celebrates when there are no looming issues and dangers. An interesting serendipity for Judah was that the neighboring nations heard of the favor of God upon them, and they wanted nothing to do with God's people, so they opted to live in peace with them. Proverbs 16:7 says, "When a man's ways please the Lord, He makes even his enemies be at peace with him." Isn't that what we all are looking for? A peaceful and fulfilling life.

What is the lesson here? God does a lot for us based upon our *heart place.* In other words, how we view Him. We are His children. Parents usually have a lot of mercy and grace for their children.

Jehoshaphat is the model of being double-minded to God's instructions and suffering for it—and being single-minded and benefiting from it. Overall, he was a strong king. He had his flaws. He missed God at times. But he always rebounded. We can learn a lot from Jehoshaphat. He walked a lot like we do today, influenced by well-meaning people who led him astray. He tried to figure things out on his own. But at the end of the day, he always came back to his Father and got wisdom and instruction. We can do the same.

IF YOUR EYE BE SINGLE

S cripture has many interesting verses. One has stood out to me through the years, and I even remember the first time I read it. I wasn't sure what it was saying, but since Jesus said it, I knew it was significant: "The light of the body is the eye: if therefore thine eye be single, thy whole body shall be full of light" (Matthew 6:22 KJV). We can say it this way as well: Your whole body is full of light when your eye becomes single.

The word *single*, used here, is speaking of being focused and deliberately working toward attaining a specific end (or goal or outcome). This verse states that the result of this single-minded determination to the Word of God is that now your body will be full of light. Light is the life of God. It is good to have light and life flowing through us.

Being in the dark usually means we don't know or understand a situation. So staying in the dark isn't a good thing. In light we see and can discern. In the darkness we cannot see; therefore, we discern nothing.

The basic premise of focusing is to pay particular attention to something. As Christians, we want to focus on what our Father has asked us to do. Where our focus goes, our actions follow. When our attention isn't focused, it becomes divided. A divided or double-minded mindset will not achieve what we want in God: "A double-minded man [is] unstable in all his ways" (James 1:8 NASB).

Doesn't that explain why many are out of money, out of ministry, out of business, and walking around defeated? Could we then say, "Our whole body is full of darkness when our eye is double"? See if this verse sheds any light on what is being said: "Whoever says he is in the Light and [yet] hates his brother [Christian, born-again child of God his Father] is in darkness even until now" (1 John 2:9).

To love our brother (or sister) is a single-minded command. If we are not walking in love toward our Christian brother, we have a "Light problem"; not loving our brother is walking in darkness. If learning to love our brother creates light, it seems we would choose to live here full-time.

The Bible says it is a light unto our path, so why are so many people not sure what God wants them to do? The answer is in Scripture, in our love walk toward other people, and in prayer time with our Father. It is in a concentrated, focused, single-minded, directed determination to know our Father. The solution comes through spending time with Him and getting to know Him.

We need to get into Scripture for ourselves. For us only. Not anyone else. To learn of Him. To know what is in Scripture so we can stay single-minded to it and stand firm in Scripture over anything we might think to the contrary.

Jesus said the Holy Spirit will lead and guide us into all truth (John 16:13). Since this is the case, wouldn't we single-mindedly let Him lead us? It seems we should follow His instruction and guidance over our own. This is what James was saying in James 1:2–8.

This makes me think of Isaiah 53, which asks "who will believe the report of the Lord," and John 12. John tells us that the people esteemed what men thought more than God. That is not having a single eye. Esteeming men, or yourself, more than

God is a double eye. A divided mind. With lip service we say we will honor God and His Word, but with our actions we follow man—or even worse, our own way.

If our view of healing is that it is for today, and it is mine, then there should be no debate about it. It will be much easier to attain. We can realize a healed body, and it can now become a reality in our lives. If our view of righteousness is that we can have a right standing with God, then we single-mindedly pursue that. We no longer visit and live with guilt and condemnation. We have focused on the desired result instead of the possibility of it not happening.

Some of us simply don't believe it can happen for us. We are conformed to the present world and situations more than we are conformed to what the Bible says about us. We are more accustomed to this world than we are to what the Word says.

There will always be drama when we follow God. The enemy of our soul will stir up all the drama he can. Everything in us will scream that this doesn't work, that we are going the wrong way and that something is not right.

However, we live by faith and not by sight. We live by faith and not by feelings. Too many times, we determine our direction based upon the ease of it, lack of resistance, or fear. Our minds want the easiest, softest route. God has called us to be more than conquerors. If we are taking the easiest route, we have conquered nothing. Defaulting to the easiest route over God's instructions for us is a double-minded mindset.

Will it be easy? No. Will it be worth it? Yes. When we stand before our Father in heaven and He says, "Well done," will that be enough? Of course it will. We have a major part to play in hearing Him say that. We can choose this day whom we will serve (Joshua 24:14). We can. Only if we choose to stay single-minded to His instructions. Only if we choose to stay single-minded to what the Word says we have, and who it says we are. We choose. That is our right. The Enemy cannot take that from us. He doesn't have that kind of power. Only we can give our rights away. Instead of surrendering our lives and wills to the flesh, with all its addictions, maybe it's time that we learn to surrender our lives and our will to God. That is a living sacrifice in His sight (see Romans 12:1).

Here is one last Scripture that I want us to consider:

And this is the message [the message of promise] which we have heard from Him and now are reporting to you: God is Light, and there is no darkness in Him at all [no, not in any way]. [So] if we say we are partakers together and enjoy fellowship with Him when we live and move and are walking about in darkness, we are [both] speaking falsely and do not live and practice the Truth [which the Gospel presents]. But if we [really] are living and walking in the Light, as He [Himself] is in the Light, we have [true, unbroken] fellowship with one another, and the blood of Jesus Christ His Son cleanses (removes) us from all sin and guilt [keeps us cleansed from sin in all its forms and manifestations]. (John 1:5–7)

These are the benefits of walking in the light, where our Father lives. Our Father is Light. To walk with Him, we have to walk in the light. So, to decide to walk in that light, with single-minded determination, is the key to this fellowship. It comes from our obedience to Him. Another serendipity of walking in this Light is that we walk in His love. The best way I know to walk in love is to walk with Jesus, in the light.

But when we say we walk with Him but are double-minded, we can easily see that we're in the dark. God doesn't live in the dark. We haven't obeyed what He's asked us to do. This is a real deception in the body of Christ today. If we want fellowship with the Father, we must love God and love our brother.

Walking in the light is acting. Walking in the dark is reacting. God is always instructing us in a way that we can act. Act on His Word. Act on His love. Act on His promises.

ACTING INSTEAD OF REACTING

Deciding to keep our eye single and therefore having our body full of light is a choice. I believe it comes down to learning to act and not react to what life throws at us.

Many of us live in a world of reacting to what comes our way. A reaction can be positive, but it can also be negative. Occasionally, very negative. When we forget to pray and seek divine instructions, we usually react to a problem. Acting comes when we take the time to seek God, get the answer, and act on the instructions given to us.

No matter the problem we are facing, the situation we are trying to solve, or the insurmountable mountain in front of us, the instructions of God will bring an answer. The instructions of God will bring life. Divine life is imparted to us. Remember, the word *instruction* here is speaking of the seed given by Father. This instruction contains divine life. Seeds are designed to do that. As a point of reference, the way I'm using the word *life* is "solution." God's instructions bring life into any situation.

God's instructions also bring light. The way I'm using *light* here is "illumination." Illumination in the spiritual realm. Illumination so we can see how our seed is being planted, so the problem doesn't seem so insurmountable. When we let Holy Spirit bring light to a situation, we act and that *action* brings life (a solution to the problem).

When we don't let Holy Spirit bring light into a situation, we are caught in darkness. This is usually where we react. The reason we are in darkness is because we are defaulting to our own way—our own reasons. We don't know how the situation will turn out, so we default to trying to bring a solution on our own. This is a normal reaction; it's called "fight or flight" by psychologists. Staying in the self-survival mode usually keeps us in darkness instead of getting His instructions. This is a sure-fire sign we are double-minded. The results usually are not what we hoped for. We are going our own way. Our eye is not single. And in many cases, reacting makes the problem much worse.

God is well aware of the human condition and our attempts at trying to navigate through this life. He knows the plans He has for us. He knows how to get us through a problem. Jeremiah 29:11 confirms this: "For I know the thoughts that I think toward you, saith the Lord, thoughts of peace, and not of evil, to give you an expected end" (KJV). There is no reaction in this verse. It's a proactive statement.

When God instructs us, all the tools we need for the endeavor are provided. He doesn't want us to fight our own circumstances. This would be reacting to a stimulus. The heavenly instructions carry all the tools we need. God wants us to look at it from His heavenly perspective, which is designed to put us in the eternal, heavenly realm instead of an earthly, "problem solving" quandary. People living in the earthly realm, looking for earthly solutions, will have a hard time getting divine results. They may have to default to His mercy for that. He is teaching us to be an "acting" force—to take the "promised land," overcome all the "giants in our land," and have an offensive mindset.

So how do we work through a problem? How do we go about getting instructions, working through those instructions, and then getting more instructions if we need them?

James 1 explains the process.

PATIENCE

J ames 1 is a pivotal section of Scripture. It is vital to understanding how to live a single-minded life. We are not getting out of the storms and the problems. There will be times when we really don't know what to do. God's wisdom is vital in those times, and changing our perspective will be beneficial.

"My brethren, count it all joy when ye fall into various trials" (James 1:2 NKJV). This verse is telling us to be joyful when we have a problem. Do we do this, though? Usually, despair, fear, concern, and worry come with a problem. But all these reactions are obvious signs of being double-minded.

James tells us to be joyful when we have a problem. Why? Because the instructions we will receive from God are *more real* than the problem. We will be able to overcome any problem because our Father has given us the answer. His eternal, divine answer is *more real* than the problem we face on this earth. The joy he is speaking of in this verse now comes because the problem is being addressed using His instructions—His single-minded, "I don't waiver," "I AM that I AM" Jehovah instructions.

Because of these instructions, we can now be joyful. We

know that He has heard us and is moving on our behalf. We are joyful because we are cared for, instructed, and being moved from a problem to a solution.

Maybe this verse will help us understand the concept: "Looking away [from all that will distract] to Jesus, Who is the leader and the Source of our faith [giving the first incentive for our belief] and is also its Finisher [bringing it to maturity and perfection]. He, *for the joy [of obtaining the prize] that was set before Him, endured the cross, despising and ignoring the shame, and is now seated at the right hand of the throne of God"* (Hebrews 12:2).

I have a saying I use when I'm overwhelmed by our Father: "Wow. Just wow." Jesus will always model for us if we let Him. He was the first to understand joy in the middle of a trial. Let us learn from Jesus so that we too can "count it all joy when we fall into various trials."

"Knowing that the testing of your faith produces patience" (James 1:3 NKJV). The King James translation interprets patience as endurance. But look at the single-minded veracity of the writer. He is telling us to be joyful when we enter into a trial or problem, speaking to us as if we know something. Insider information, if you will. Our faith can be measured by how patient we are. Strong faith can be measured by the level of patience and calm we operate in.

The writer here is saying that since we know we are getting the answer because our Father has instructed us, we need to relax. The answer is on the way. We can literally measure what we believe, how single-minded we are, and where we operate in God, by our level of peace. How deeply we embrace that the problem has been taken care of is indicated by our patience. Peace demonstrates the level of patience we are walking in.

A double-minded person is not at peace. They are worrying. They are staring at the problem, and so it becomes bigger. God's single-minded word is designed to overcome our problems. God's single-minded word is designed to put us in a place of peace. With that peace, we are able to rest, receive, and watch God move.

What is a miracle, then?

A miracle is when God divinely takes something away or changes it. He supernaturally does something for us out of His goodness. I love miracles. I believe in them. But I see no one learning from a miracle. Yes, we are thankful, but I see us becoming stronger and changing the world only as we become single-minded to our Father's instructions.

Let's look into patience a bit more. "But let patience have *its* perfect work, that you may be perfect and complete, lacking nothing" (v. 4 NKJV). Patience has a perfecting work. *Perfect* here means "maturing work." In other words, we'll become mature. So the verse could be read "But let patience have her maturing work." Patience is a sign of maturity. This is also the discerning of good and evil spoken of in Hebrews 5.

We are patient because we have heard from God. His answer to the problem speaks louder in our hearts than the current issue facing us. Remember David, when he heard the giant yelling at the army of God and said, "Who is this uncircumcised Philistine?" God's word was more real to David than a giant ranting and raving across the valley. A word from the Lord is more effective in solving a problem than anything else. James's words "wanting nothing" tell us that it is possible to live in no fear, no concern, no doubt. We become like Jesus, who modeled for us what it meant to walk on the water, calm the sea, raise the dead, and do the works of the Father.

Patience, in itself, has a maturing work. Since we know we can't fail because we have been given the solution, this ultimately becomes the reality in our life instead of the problem. We are now operating in the "light" that we discussed in chapter 8.

"If any of you lack wisdom, let him ask of God, who gives to all liberally and without reproach; and it will be given to him" (v. 5 NKJV). I absolutely love this verse. Oh, the kindness of God. Oh, the goodness of God. What is it saying? That there will be times when we lack the wisdom to solve a problem. The situation may be so overwhelming that we can't hear God. We are paralyzed by fear and concern. We're not able to make rational decisions. But He gives instructions to us, as many as we need. This gives us the opportunity to be single-minded until we get to where we have an absolute answer. Not an "I hope so" but a solid "build your house on the rock" answer.

Let's say we are faced with a dire situation. We pray and hear God, or we find a portion of Scripture that covers and addresses this problem. But the situation is overwhelming and we lose our way in the struggle and torment of the problem. What now?

Consider Peter walking on the water. He saw Jesus walking on the water and wanted to do the same. Peter said, "Lord, if it is you, bid me come." What did Jesus say? What were His single-minded instructions? "Come."

Peter got out of the boat and went to Jesus. But as he was walking toward Jesus, he became double-minded by looking at the situation: the boisterous waves. We shouldn't be too quick to judge Peter here. If we've struggled with a problem, we have no room to judge. He walked on the water. Let's learn to do the same. This fifth verse in James is saying that Peter could have asked Jesus for more instructions. Peter didn't though. He was overwhelmed by the enormousness of the problem. Sound familiar?

Notice something else here. Peter was probably saying something like this: "Lord, I'm fearful. What do I do?" Jesus reached out to Peter and said, "Why do you have little faith?" What if we read it like this: "Peter, you were single-minded because you asked me if you could come to Me on the water. I single-mindedly answered you and said, 'Come.' You became double-minded because you looked at the waves. When you became double-minded, you started to sink."

Jesus's instructions are designed to rescue us. This is the love of the Father. When James says that God will give us abundant instructions, what that means is that He will continue to tell us what we need to do until we embrace our answer. He tells us again and again, until the instructions become clear. We could also say until we become single-minded with His answer. Then our single-minded resolve becomes our reality. The benefit of that single-minded resolve is that we now live in the realm of patience. We long for peace instead of running from our problems in fear.

"But let him ask in faith, without doubting. For he who doubts is like a wave of the sea driven and tossed by the wind" (v. 6 NKJV). There are two interesting points to observe here. First, faith is a single-minded act. The first part of the verse could be stated this way: "But let him ask in faith single-mindedly. No double-minded allowed." This is a sure, confident place in God. We know it is impossible to please God without faith (Hebrews 11:6). God, who is single-minded, is always in the position of faith. This is often the reason that answers to prayer don't come. We have moved from the single-minded position we had with Him in prayer, and fallen into a position of wavering, second-guessing, "I am not too sure I will survive it this time" thinking pattern. We are out of position to receive from God.

The second point is emphatic truth. If we waiver, become double-minded, we are unstable. The trial has overtaken us. Scripture describes the ocean being driven by the wind. The ocean is unstable in high winds when the storms are of a hurricane magnitude. Our lives become like these ocean storms. The wind of the problem is driving the peace and answers away from us. Perhaps fear and concern take our peace. We are so unsettled that we can no longer hear from our Father. Our mind now sees the worst possible scenario. There is no hope. We are manifesting fear, doubt, worry, and anxiety. This is when God's goodness and mercy come into play.

We have become like the disciples caught in the storm in the boat (see chapter 5). The storm in our lives is now so strong that we have forgotten the instructions from Holy Spirit. Those life-giving instructions have become a vague memory. We cry out,

"Don't you care that we perish?" The confidence that came with single-minded peace has left. We are tossed like the waves in a sea of torment.

"For let not that man suppose that he will receive anything from the Lord" (v. 7 NKJV). This is a powerful verse. Double-minded instability limits our ability to receive from God. It paralyzes us so we can't access the Source of our answer. This verse confirms that we receive nothing from the Lord because we have become double-minded. We have now become a problem.

Why are we the problem? Because God only responds to faith. He only responds to our faith. This is repeated throughout Scripture and is not debatable. When the problem overcomes us, as stated in verse 6, our instability causes us to be moved—to lose our position and not stay fixed and stable. We are truly the wave of the sea that is tossed.

God says, "I am the LORD, I change not" (Malachi 3:6 KJV). He heard our prayer and sent us an answer. He heard our prayer and sent us a truth, His word. We are the ones who have moved off that answer. The wind—our problem—has knocked us off course. We are no longer stable. We have become a moving target. When we move, we move from the answer. We move from the solution, and from His provision. He is not withholding the answer or solution from us; we have moved away from it. Our double-mindedness has made us move from the stability, the answer, the single-mindedness. We have now moved to instability. Anything that is not of faith is sin. Evil. Thank God for grace and mercy.

"*he is* a double-minded man, unstable in all his way." (v. 8 NKJV). Simple enough. Not much explanation needed. But do look at the instability in "all our ways." Problems overwhelm us. Disease and sickness overwhelm us. They take over every area of our life. We are no longer stable in *any* area of our life.

A rebellious child, on drugs and living on the street, can overwhelm our job performance. It can limit our ability to sleep, and our interaction with friends and family becomes hindered.

Having a child attempt suicide brings the worst fear to our minds. We pray it doesn't become a reality. It consumes our every thought. A cancer diagnosis stops our world. So does a project imploding at work. A car wreck. Sudden death in the family. All of these things can prematurely age us. All of these things can paralyze our daily lives. The trials and traumas can make us unstable in all our ways.

God always has the answer, but He gets blamed for many things. Most of the time He has nothing to do with what happens in our lives. We are the ones who stray from His instructions. We are the ones who depart from His word and go our own way.

He is trying to remedy a situation for us. When we determine to go our own way, we box Him into where He is hindered in moving for us. He doesn't violate the free will that He has given to us. Yes, He has mercy and grace in times of need, but His best is to lead us out of our problems. (I know this is debatable and hard to read. But I asked you to consider it in the first chapter. Just consider. All I ask.)

Look at this Scripture: "You will guard him and keep him in perfect and constant peace whose mind [both its inclination and its character] is stayed on You, because he commits himself to You, leans on You, and hopes confidently in You" (Isaiah 26:3). This amazing verse is the single-minded message we have been speaking of in this book. It is the key to staying in peace during every storm of life.

God's peace can be our anchor. His peace *should* be our anchor. This verse makes it plain. By keeping our minds stayed on what God says, instead of on the problem, we're able to break through to the solution. Keeping our minds focused on Him positions us to receive the answer more easily. On the other hand, looking at the circumstances will only give us doubt, fear, and torment.

Hope and excitement come when we are patient through a problem. We know our faith is working. We know He heard us and brought us an answer. We can now do what Jesus did when He was faced with a problem: we can rest in the back of the boat as He did in Mark 4. We are single-minded as He was, in total peace. Isaiah 26 tells us to keep our mind stayed on Him—on the answer He has given to us, on the verses of promise in Scripture, and on the leading by Holy Spirit.

To finish this chapter, let's look at this passage of Scripture again in *THE MESSAGE*:

Consider it a sheer gift, friends, when tests and challenges come at you from all sides. You know that under pressure, your faith life is forced into the open and shows its true colors. So don't try to get out of anything prematurely. Let it do its work so you become mature and well-developed, not deficient in any way. If you don't know what you're doing, pray to the Father. He loves to help. You'll get his help, and won't be condescended to when you ask for it. Ask boldly, believingly, without a second thought. People who "worry their prayers" are like wind-whipped waves. Don't think you're going to get anything from the Master that way, adrift at sea, keeping all your options open. (James 1:2–8 MSG)

MY GREAT AWAKENING

I have carried the single-minded revelation for well over ten years, and received more clarification on it at the end of 2017 and the beginning of 2018. It seemed like I shared it time and time again but no one heard me. I'd taught Mark 4 so many times that my Bible just fell open to the portion where Jesus crosses over to the other side.

As of this writing, the Lord never has let me teach the actual parable, though I have tried many times, to no avail. He would always shift me from wanting to teach that parable, to a single-minded example somewhere else in the Word. I have no idea why, but I do know my job is to listen to Him and be single-minded to His instructions.

I have been teaching the single-minded revelation at His Outpouring, my church in Wyoming. Our congregation/family has begun to understand it and use it in their everyday lives. We use an open-forum preaching style, which means people can stop me at any point and ask a question or make a comment. In the open-forum preaching style, most answers to my questions fall back to either being single- or double-minded. Either we are single-minded to His instructions or we aren't.

While teaching in front of a congregation in Canada, I heard myself saying these words: "The reason Holy Spirit would not release the revelation of single- and double-minded was because I had not walked in enough love for others at that point in my ministry." *This is the only reason the single-minded revelation was in limbo?* I thought.

When I heard Holy Spirit say that, I was as surprised as anyone in the congregation that night. It made total sense. The light came on. Revelation really needs to be wrapped in love. If the revelation isn't released in love, the message is lost because people will come under condemnation. It really isn't about correcting the congregation; that is Holy Spirit's job. Our job is to model Jesus—to do it the way He did.

I don't try to get someone delivered. I choose to love them and then the deliverance is a byproduct. Same with salvation. It's much easier to lead someone into becoming born again when they know they are being loved. When you love people, you don't take their dignity. Dignity is important to all of us. Jesus never took anyone's dignity. Religion doesn't care; it'll never be concerned about dignity.

I now see why a lot of revelation we have received is not released to the body of Christ. The revelation may be exactly what the body needs and would benefit from; however, without love, God's goodness cannot come through. And the goodness of God brings men to repentance (Romans 2:4). We've had enough guilt and condemnation taught from the pulpit for three lifetimes. Yes, it may be a needed revelation, but the person delivering the message may be needing more time to learn how to prefer his brother more than himself (see Romans 12:10). In other words, how to walk in love toward others.

I am not advocating the toleration of sin. I am not looking past blatant rebellion. I do not encourage promiscuity in the church. I believe in moral purity in the personal lives of those who minister. I have simply found a place of compassion that draws people who are terribly lost, hurting, and double-minded to come to God. This is a place where they actually make a change. If we shun them from the church, how will they ever hear?

I was on a long fast when Holy Spirit visited me one night. The visitation started at one a.m. and went until three a.m. Two hours! Electrical, anointed impulses shot through my body as I lay in a fetal position. Holy Spirit kept saying to me over and over, "Love My children." Three hundred times. (I say three hundred times because it just kept going.) I would get a release and then He would say it again. All this time my body jolted with pure Holy Spirit power. I thought it was never going to end. I was past the point of exhaustion. He kept saying it—over and over—"Love My children."

When the experience finally subsided, I was on my side and drenched in sweat. Tired, worn out, and shell-shocked. I was a mess. But I'd started to understand that it wasn't about me. It was about His children. How can we love God, whom we don't see, and not love our brother, whom we do see (see 1 John 4:20)?

I had a major dose of His perspective invade my soul and life that night. I wasn't the same. I no longer looked at people for what they could do for me. I was no longer disappointed by people just because I saw the potential they walked in that they chose to waste. Hurting people hurt people. Lying people will lie to you.

Do you understand what I'm saying? It isn't about us and our feelings. We have to get past that. I was learning to no longer be disappointed by people who caused me harm. I was starting to look at them through Jesus's eyes. People who are hurting act broken. That is why they have the potential to hurt others. In my opinion, it is not the intent of a broken person to harm others. It happens because they are hurt.

After seeing His children from His perspective, I found my desire to follow Jesus was now much stronger. Fear of man and what he might think was dying. I was about my Father's business. The things I had always wanted to do for God were now happening. Helping others was no longer a burden to me but a joy. The fear of sharing the gospel with others was gone. The desire to pray and help people become better was now my main motivation for living. I was a changed man. I only wanted to see people the way God did. I wanted to see people with the same kind of love that our Father had.

A couple of weeks later, close to the end of a fifty-day fast, I heard Holy Spirit speak softly. It was the sweetest, most unassuming voice. He said, "Come up higher." He said it only three times. I wasn't overly excited. Instead, I felt a deep responsibility. The thought of coming up higher in Him meant I could no longer be who I was. He was expecting more from me. He trusted me.

While those are words we all want to hear, while they are the words I had fasted, prayed, and cried out for, now there was a difference. They were no longer my main motivation. The promotion and exaltation I had longed for were now in a safe place in my life. It wasn't the main reason I was in the ministry. It was a byproduct of spending time with Jesus and being washed in His love. It now was no longer about me but about His children. I was learning to love His children. He could now trust me with being able to "come up higher." It was now about coming up higher in His kingdom, not in my ministry.

I was pondering that as I stood in front of this congregation in Canada. I saw something. Most of us ask three hundred times if Holy Spirit will promote us. We ask three hundred times for Him to give us revival, three hundred times for an anointing to go about doing His work, three hundred times. But why don't we ask three hundred times for the ability to love His children? I was guilty of that. I wanted an anointing and the power of God in my life, but Holy Spirit surprised me and turned it around.

Isn't this the missing key to a great move of God? Isn't it being about our Father's business? Isn't it about the glory going to Him? It seems we want the anointing, revival, and presence so we can be known for carrying the power of God. I saw something on that long fast: the glory belongs to Him. I don't want glory here on this earth. I only want to please my heavenly Father.

The wonderful thing about following Holy Spirit and staying single-minded is that we can stay in the perfect will of our Father. We can now *know* that we are where we're supposed to be. No more guessing. No more chasing after what others have. No more begging and pleading. Instead, we follow the instructions from Holy Spirit so we can be about His business. I want to be where He has placed me. I want that confidence. I want to hear the words "Well done."

If you want a ministry, love people. If you want a better business, love people. If you want to carry His power and anointing, love people. If you want your children delivered and off drugs, love people. Jesus came to save the world. He came to deliver and heal the lost. If you want His heart, love people. If you want His power, love people. If you want to carry revival, love people.

Loving people is the best possible area to put single-mindedness to work. I would suggest going after God with all your heart. I would hang around with Him until the byproduct of that time is loving people. We become like who we hang with. Become single-minded in knowing God. Abandon yourself to spending as much time as possible with Him. Learn to love people.

There was a period in my life where I would spend many hours a day in His presence. Was the price too high? No. I wanted to model Jesus. I wanted to do the greater works of which He spoke. I wanted what He said I could have. The greatest thing Jesus modeled was His love for people. He laid His life down to love people. Not just on the cross but in his day-to-day interactions. He single-mindedly followed Holy Spirit's instructions.

Holy Spirit will always lead you to love His children. We should not have and do ministry without His reason for ministry. What is His reason for ministry? To put you on stage or in a pulpit? To make you a household name? I don't think so. I believe you'll find the answer is in loving His people—the people He came to heal, find, and restore.

We have spoken a lot about learning to love people. Now let's look at it in a fresh way. Maybe in a single-minded way.

IT ALL WORKS BY LOVE

I t all works by love. Is that true, really? We know that many books have been written on the subject of walking in love. Many sermons have been taught on it. I've even preached a few sermons on love myself. Is it possible that "walking in love" has become a trigger statement? You know, something we've heard that we assume we understand, but at the end of the day, we really seem to come up short in truly walking in it.

I believe it has. Why do we glaze over it in our daily lives? We know that we need to honor the commandment to walk in love, but do we really know how to do it? It seems that our attempts to walk in it often fall short. Is this an indicator that we may not really understand it? We have heard that God is love. We have heard that faith works by love. So is there something we're missing?

I'm not talking about the kind of love we have for our children or spouse. Not the kind of love we have for people who are kind to us. Not the kind of thing we do after being inspired to do so by a moving sermon. This isn't only about being nice to people. It isn't only about biting our tongue when we have the right to tell someone off. What is it, then, this "walking in love" thing?

In Scripture, several different Greek words can be translated by the one English word *love*. The most common four words used at the time of the Bible was written are *stergo, phileo, eros,* and *agape*. We use the concept behind these words when we talk about love in our daily lives, so let's look at a quick definition of each word.

Stergo is a love for the members of one's own family. It might be used when talking about the love between a parent and child. This term for love might also be used for the affection toward a family pet. It could be thought of as devotion toward someone related. Interesting to note here that this word is only used twice in the New Testament—in Romans 1:31 and 2 Timothy 3:3, where Paul is saying that people will be without even natural familial devotion.

Phileo can be seen as the type of love shared between friends. This is the word used in James 2:23 describing Abraham as a "friend of God." It is also used as a compound word in 2 Timothy 3 and translated "lover of self," "lover of money," "not loving good," "lover of pleasure," and "lover of God." This form of love is based on mutual experience. While it is a deep affection for another, it is based on the shared experience of that love and does not have the element of sacrificial giving that we will find when we define *agape*.

Eros is the third kind of love. This Greek word is not used in the Bible but is found elsewhere in the Greek literature of that time period. Eros is the sensual, self-satisfying, self-pleasing of one's sexual appetite. Even in the context of sex in marriage as addressed in Scripture, this flesh-based concept of love is not presented. In fact, in Ephesians 5:25, where Paul is admonishing husbands to love their wives, the word *agape* is used.

Finally, *agape* has been defined by many as the "God-kind of love," and indeed it is. However, we need to think more about what that really means.

I remember preaching in a church many years ago. The pastor was a good friend of mine, and he introduced me to the congregation like this: "Brad is going to teach on love today. He doesn't walk in it, but he is going to teach it." He was making a joke, but I was thinking, *He really isn't too far off on that assumption.* Suffice it to say, I had heard about the need to walk in love.

Is there a way to determine if we are really walking in love or just giving lip service? Again, I believe Scripture is clear on this. There is a definite way to gauge our love walk, and I believe it is much more than focusing on being nice to others or trying to be agreeable. That's important, but there's more to consider. I'll give you four verses out of John. John is known as the disciple whom Jesus loved. Let's seriously consider what he records Jesus as saying:

If you [really] love Me, you will keep (obey) My commands. (John 14:15)

The person who has My commands and keeps them is the one who [really] loves Me, and whoever [really] loves Me will be loved by My Father, and I [too] will love him and will show (reveal, manifest) Myself to him. [I will let Myself be clearly seen by him and make Myself real to him]. (John 14:21)

Jesus answered, If a person [really] loves Me, he will keep My word [obey My teaching]; and My Father will love him, and We will come to him and make Our home (abode, special dwelling place) with him. Anyone who does not [really] love Me does not observe *and* obey My teaching. And the teaching which you hear *and* heed is not Mine, but [comes] from the Father Who sent Me. (John 14:23–24)

Jesus had stated many times in this chapter that "if you love Me, you will keep My commandments." Does that sound like a single-minded instruction? I believe so. Jesus obviously was single-minded to the instructions he received from His Father. With that in mind, we need to consider and do what Jesus is saying here.

And what is the true test of walking in love? How we treat and act toward our brother. Walking with God at this level will automatically give us His perspective. What is His perspective? To seek and save those who are lost. If I am in my Father's business, I'm going to become actively involved in that business. I'm going to help Him seek and save those who are lost. I'm going to get His perspective. I'm going to see the value in people who were created by Him and whom He loves dearly. I'm going to love them the way He does. I'm going to walk in love with my brother. I'm going to walk in love with God's creation. He has asked me to do it, and I will do it with a single-minded resolve.

These verses plainly tell us that obedience to Father's instruction is the way we show our love for Him. So, is he also saying that not following His instructions shows that we haven't mastered the love walk? I think so. Not an easy pill to swallow, but I'm tired of not knowing the truth. I don't want to assume anymore.

Walking in double-mindedness would be choosing to walk our own way instead of following His instructions. Could our desire to walk our own way indicate that there are areas in our lives we need to reflect on and make corrections to? Would those corrections help us be single-minded and learn that following Him *is* walking in love? Wouldn't we then want to walk as Jesus did and keep our Father's commands? Could it be that simple?

I know that isn't an easy concept to grasp. How can simply being obedient to God show the level of love I have for the kingdom? I reflect on it a lot. I reflect on it when I'm not wanting to follow anymore. When I want to go my own way. When things aren't working out as I thought they would and I want to throw in the towel and quit. When everyone seems to be turning against me.

I have to do what the disciples did on the boat when it was

full of water. When it looks like I missed God and I'm out there on my own making a mess of things. I'm learning to go to Jesus, free of guilt and condemnation, and say to Him, "Am I doing the right thing, Jesus? Please tell me one more time what to do." I seriously believe it's that simple.

Look at what Jesus is telling us in John 14: "Put your money where your mouth is. Show Me your love by your obedience to Me. Stop looking at the circumstances and your empty checkbook. Quit looking at your sick body. Quit looking at what isn't working in your life. Look at Me and My Word. Put the Word of God in the place of priority in your life."

A mature believer is one who walks in love. A mature believer is one who knows how to be obedient to heavenly instructions. A mature believer is one who knows how to discern good and evil. A mature believer is one who lives in the heavenly realm— the realm of fellowshipping and following Father.

Now, with that in mind, let's look at one of the most familiar portions of Scripture: the Ten Commandments. They were given to a generation that was bound up in the sinful nature. This generation had no one to redeem them yet. The sacrifice of bulls and goats, to cover their sins, was only good for a year. The high priest was the only one who could stand in the place of redemption for them. Only an annual sacrifice. Jesus, the eternal sacrifice, had not yet come or even been revealed.

The Ten Commandments, from the Old Testament, are fulfilled by two basic commands in the New Testament, so let's consider what they are saying. These two commandments replace the other ten. New illumination is shed on us by observing them, and understanding them will bring real liberty into our lives.

They are something we can do. It may not be easy, but they are still doable.

THE TWO COMMANDS

The Ten Commandments are found in Exodus 20:1–17. Now in the book of Matthew, an expert in Jewish law asked Jesus a question as He was teaching: "What is the greatest command?"

Master, which is the great commandment in the law? Jesus said unto him, *Thou shalt love the Lord thy God with all thy heart, and with all thy soul, and with all thy mind.* This is the first and great commandment. And the second is like unto it, *Thou shalt love thy neighbor as thyself.* On these two commandments hang all the law and the prophets. (Matthew 22:36–40 KJV)

Jesus answered by breaking the commandments into two parts: the first four commandments of the ten are summed up by "love the Lord thy God," and the next six commandments can be summed up as "love thy neighbor as thyself." So these are the two commandments we're to follow. Following these two automatically fulfills the ten. Again, they are love God and love His children.

I hear people preach that there are three commands. The one they are addressing as *the third* is where the verse states "love thy neighbor as thyself." I won't call it a commandment, but I do see the logic in it. This verse is telling us to love ourselves. It is hard to give something away until we possess it first.

The best way to love ourselves is to let God touch us. Letting Him touch us means we are in His presence. Wanting to please Him comes from being obedient to what He asks us to do. I believe that living in God's presence on a daily basis is vital. Wanting to please Him is also vital. Our perspective can move to an eternal perspective by being around an eternal God. In this place of being in His presence, we start to love, which is eternal.

Here is a post I put on Facebook not too long ago. I think it covers what these verses are saying. I still look at this post and consider it often:

Consider this, it's not a faith struggle. It really isn't. It is a love strug-

gle. Do you love others more than yourself? Or, do you love God more than yourself? It's not about loving yourself really or not loving yourself, it's just preferring your brother above yourself. It's preferring what Holy Ghost wants above your opinion. That's where the drama comes in and struggles. When we try to Self-preserve. Self-preservation is just this: we don't think we're going to get ours. "Jesus preserving" is this: you are going to get the byproduct of Jesus's love, and it is so much more than anything you could ask or imagine. Prefer Jesus above you. In THAT "preferring," others get blessed. And you? Well, you get peace. You can judge your peace by who you prefer. Put others first today. Put Jesus first today. Quit thinking about you and your rights. Give this one a test drive. See if I'm right.

Looking again at these verses in Matthew 22, we are told to love the Lord our God with all our heart, soul, and mind. This is a decision-making process we can control. It is a choice we make. We learned from the chapter on good and evil (chapter 4) that a mature Christian is one who can follow the leading of Holy Spirit. We are instructed here, by Jesus, in Matthew 22, that following God's instructions is our way of showing God our love for Him. So we can now surmise that a mature Christian is one who walks in obedience to God's instructions. The serendipity of this is that we now walk in love as a result of that obedience. Interesting how all that works.

So if we show our love and maturity by, yet again, following His instructions, wouldn't we also show our love and maturity for Him by discerning the difference between good and evil? Wow. Do you see that? This ties in so strongly with the greater works in John 14. (I'm not going into the greater works in this book. There will be a future book for that.) Can it really be this simple?

I used to think that learning to walk in love was hard. That it was something that only a Mother Teresa type of person could do. I really worked at it. I'm sure you have too. When I determined that today is my day to walk in love, usually everything that could go wrong did. It seemed everyone was angry with me.

It seemed as if my day was falling apart. Did I unleash something negative in my life?

So my question for us is this: Can learning to live in the divine life automatically get us to the place where we truly prefer our brother? I know that we become like those whom we fellowship with. And I know the easiest way to be like God is to hang with Him. So when He instructs us and helps us through a problem, isn't that one of the ways He spends time with us? This time with Him would give us His knowledge and instruction. It would let us discover Him in His word and Scripture. It would teach us to act and operate the way He does.

I believe that following His instructions demonstrates that I am learning how to love His children. How we feel, at any particular moment, should not dictate following His voice or a portion of revelation we have received from Scripture. People today tend to be so moved by feelings. But following our feelings too closely will not lead us to do much for God. If we don't feel like obeying our Father, how can we accomplish His will on this earth? If we're going to become mature in Christ, we have to seriously put our feelings in check.

God is an emotional being who loves us dearly, but He moves for us according to His Word. He created our emotions, but He is moved by our faith. Faith in His Word. I love emotions as much as anyone else; they make life worth living. But we cannot let them totally control our life. The world lives in this emotional realm. We are supposed to come out of the world. We are now in the kingdom. Shouldn't we learn to function in kingdom faith?

If we want to walk in God's will, we will follow His Word. God's will is His Word. Additionally, Matthew 24:35 tells us, "Heaven and earth will pass away, but my words will never pass away" (NIV). He is a faith-God. He is teaching us faith as He guides and directs us. This is true faith. His faith.

When I described the three hundred times God told me to "love My children," that was not a suggestion from Him. It was an instruction to further His kingdom on earth. Holy Spirit wants to fix situations in the world. When are we going to take part in the solution instead of the problem? To be part of the solution is to honor what we are told in the Word of God.

Let me share a secret that will speed us up in our Christian walk and save us a lot of frustration in the kingdom of God: Love His children. Don't take this lightly. Follow this commandment in Matthew 22. Make it a priority. We don't love people because they are nice to us. We don't love people because they love us back. We don't love people because they are lovely to us. We love people because He has instructed us to.

If anyone says, I love God, and hates (detests, abominates) his brother [in Christ], he is a liar; for he who does not love his brother, whom he has seen, cannot love God, Whom he has not seen. And this command (a charge, order, injunction) we have from Him: that he who loves God shall love his brother [believer] also. (1 John 4:20–21)

That is an eye-opener. We can't proclaim our love of God if we aren't showing that love for people. It is a command as well as an instruction. It all works by love. It has to. This earth realm has not been love-motivated. It is a lesser kingdom. It is about self, pride, arrogance, getting more, and profiting selfishly. The kingdom of God is about rescuing the lost—our brothers and sisters. If you want to prosper in this life, make rescuing the lost a priority. The byproduct is you'll have peace with God. You'll learn to love people as well.

Consider this, from CNN Interactive's *World News*:

"Mother Teresa was aware of this criticism," spoken against her. "She would shrug as if saying, 'While you go on discussing causes and explanations, I will kneel beside the poorest of the poor and attend to their needs.' People from all walks of life crowded along both sides of the 5 kilometers (3.1 miles) procession route, which took her body from St. Thomas Church, where she had been lying in state for the past week."[1]

A 3.1-mile procession at her funeral! Imagine it.

When are we going to get what she had? When are we going to become obedient and follow His instructions? One more time, the love of God makes us single-minded. When we decide that we have options contrary to what He has told us, we become double-minded. A double-minded man will receive nothing from the Lord (see James 1:7–8). Now consider Matthew 5:43–48:

You have heard that it was said, You shall love your neighbor and hate your enemy; But I tell you, Love your enemies and pray for those who persecute you, To show that you are the children of your Father Who is in heaven; for He makes His sun rise on the wicked and on the good, and makes the rain fall upon the upright and the wrongdoers [alike]. For if you love those who love you, what reward can you have? Do not even the tax collectors do that? And if you greet only your brethren, what more than others are you doing? Do not even the Gentiles (the heathen) do that? You, therefore, must be perfect [growing into complete maturity of godliness in mind and character, having reached the proper height of virtue and integrity], as your heavenly Father is perfect.

Look at verse 48. It just won't go away, will it? It states that we are to be *perfect*. Perfect in that verse is about the process of becoming mature. But perfect, or mature in that verse, also would be about discerning good and evil. Perfect in that verse is also about obeying Father's commands and loving our brother. Perfect in that verse is also about becoming single-minded.

Now let's take a look at our will and how to make it work for us. How do we line up our will with Father's will? There's a New Testament story that I believe aptly shows an excellent way to be determined to follow God.

RESOLVE

Resolve is defined as "deciding firmly on a course of action."[1] Another dictionary defines it this way: "As a noun, resolve refers to a strong determination to do something."[2] This entire book is about hearing God and doing as He instructs. This is what Jesus modeled for us. It is the place of stability in our lives. We can see it in detail in Hebrews 12:1–4:

> Therefore we also, since we are surrounded by so great a
> cloud of witnesses, let us lay aside every weight, and the
> sin which so easily ensnares *us,* and let us run with
> endurance the race that is set before us, looking unto
> Jesus, the author and finisher of *our* faith, who for the joy
> that was set before Him endured the cross, despising the
> shame, and has sat down at the right hand of the throne
> of God. For consider Him who endured such hostility
> from sinners against Himself, lest you become weary and
> discouraged in your souls. You have not yet resisted to
> bloodshed, striving against sin. (NKJV)

Deciding to do as we are instructed by Holy Spirit still falls in our court. It still becomes our decision. God will never take our will. He doesn't force us to love Him and follow Him, unlike the devil who attempts to continually force his will on us daily. His attempts to kill, steal, and destroy seem to never stop. Thus, the reason we need the wisdom of God and to hear Him on a daily basis.

Before I go any further in this chapter, I want to make a quick point on the subject of resolve. I'm not using it as a motivational tool, and I'm not talking about walking something out with willpower in the natural realm. I'm using it in the fashion Holy Spirit taught me, and that is simply not letting anything in this world get in the way of our obedience to instructions given to us by our Father. But not only not letting anything get in our way, but also moving in a very decided and determined path to obedience to our Father. That obedience demonstrates that we are a son or daughter that Holy Spirit can depend on.

The world talks about working hard and "leaving it all on the field." This model is the way to succeed in this world. It works. I can attest to it. But we have Holy Spirit. He is working in our lives. He is leading us through this life. I believe we should be as diligent in following Him as the world is at following their dreams and desires. To me, pleasing God should become our ultimate dream and desire.

Consider this: I believe the church is entering the best time to serve our Father. I believe and see a positive attitude in the church about winning this world. My opinion is that some of the greatest miracles to ever occur are coming upon us. I think great church history will be made in the next few years.

One day, as I was driving down the street in Tulsa, I posed a question to the Lord. I asked Him why we never seem to have revival and moves of God like the old-timers of the faith did. I wasn't talking about Abraham or Moses (though that would be appropriate) but about the revivalist of our recent moves: William Branham, Oral Roberts, AA Allen, Maria Woodworth-Etter, or Smith Wigglesworth, to name a few.

God responded almost immediately, which excited me. He

seemed like He was more than happy to answer that question, and in fast order. He said to me, "Your generation doesn't understand what resolve means. The old-timers and the people of faith listed in Hebrews 11 did."

I didn't get upset or defensive. I mean, God answered me. I couldn't complain and say, "He didn't reach out to me." I considered what He said. He gave me a seed, which is a *rhema* word, so I studied the concept of resolve in Scripture. The result of that study created a tape series.

While writing this book, I was awakened one morning and instructed to write this chapter on resolve. I am so amazed at our Father. His thoughts are so much higher than ours. Resolve fits perfectly in this book. I believe having resolve has to be a part of our lives if we expect to have stability in the things of God.

That study back then led me to a place where I found the word *resolve* in the Bible: Luke 16:1-10. This is the story of the unjust steward and how he handled his problem when he was in trouble with his master. A steward is a person who has the authority to make decisions on behalf of his boss or company. Dealing with a steward, in this context, would be the same as dealing with the authority directly. A steward would be called a manager today.

Let's consider the unjust steward's resolve.

And he also said to his disciples, "There was a certain rich man who had a steward, and an accusation was brought to him that this man was wasting his goods. So he called him and said unto him, 'What is it that I hear about you? Give an account of your stewardship, for you can no longer be steward.' "Then the steward said within himself, 'What shall I do? For my master is taking the stewardship away from me. I cannot dig; I am ashamed to beg. I have resolved what to do, that when I am put out of the stewardship, they may receive me into their houses.' "So he called every one of his master's debtors to *him*, and said to the first, 'How much do you owe my master?' And he said, 'A hundred measures of oil.' So he said to him, 'Take your bill, and sit down quickly, and write fifty.' Then said he to another, 'And how much do you owe?' So he said, 'A hundred measures of wheat'. And he said unto him, 'Take your bill, and write eighty.' So the master commended the unjust steward because he had dealt shrewdly. For the sons of this world are more shrewd in their generation than the sons of light. "And I say to you, make friends for yourselves by unrighteous mammon, that when you fail, they may receive you into an everlasting home. He who is faithful in *what* is least is faithful also in much: and he who is unjust in what is least is unjust also in much. (Luke 16:1–10 NKJV)

Note that I'm emphasizing the resolve of the unjust steward. I am not looking at the fact that he was "unjust" but what we can learn from his example of resolve. Even though he's not an example of integrity, he is an example of staying authentic to himself and to deciding on a course of action and following it through without wavering. He was single-minded.

Let's take this verse by verse.

"And he also said to his disciples, "There was a certain rich man who had a steward, and an accusation was brought to him that this man was wasting his goods.""

(v. 1). Jesus started the parable of the unjust steward by stating that the steward had wasted his goods. In modern language, the manager stole from his boss. He embezzled. The master discovered what the steward had been doing, and the steward was not in a good position with his boss and knew it.

"So he called him and said unto him, 'What is it that I hear about you? Give an account of your stewardship, for you can no longer be steward." (v. 2). Then the steward's master called him in. The master wanted to know if what he was hearing about the steward was true. "Are you stealing from me?" Again, not a good place. This must have been a pretty blatant case though, because Jesus didn't say that he denied anything. Most thieves would deny it, I believe. The evidence against him must have been pretty convincing.

"Then the steward said within himself, 'What shall I do? For my master is taking the stewardship away from me. I cannot dig; I am ashamed to beg" (v. 3). The steward, at this point, was sure he would be dismissed from his position. And like us, he was trying to consider his options. He wasn't sure what to do. When he said he couldn't "dig or beg," I believe he was stating his qualifications. He was a negotiator, and wouldn't get another job in the same position with another employer because he was a convicted thief. No one hires a thief. (Except Jesus, who let Judas be one of the twelve to fulfill prophecy. Nothing scares Jesus.)

"I have resolved what to do, that when I am put out of the stewardship, they may receive me into their houses." (v. 4). Here we go. Decision made! No more wavering and trying to figure it out. He was good at negotiating. He knew that if he used his skill—and used it with resolve—he would get a job after he was dismissed from his current one. His resolve was so strong that he wouldn't do anything else but negotiate. It was what he did. He loved money. Money was his god, so there was no debate. He was resolved to serve his greed god and follow this god's instructions. Those instructions were to negotiate with extreme resolve.

"So he called every one of his master's debtors to *him*, and said to the first, 'How much do you owe my master?" (v. 5). Notice here, he was starting to negotiate under his master's authority. He was in trouble with his master, but he used the authority given to him and used it before it was taken away. He didn't delay to act. Look at something here: he went from reacting to acting. When he became resolved and started his course of action to survive, he was now acting.

"And he said, 'A hundred measures of oil.' So he said to him, 'Take your bill, and sit down quickly, and write fifty.' Then said he to another, 'And how much do you owe?' So he said, 'A hundred measures of wheat'. And he said unto him, 'Take your bill, and write eighty." (vv. 6–7). The steward was bold. Brazenly bold. These men owed his master a bill. He was telling them, and quickly, "I'll give you a tremendous discount if you pay the bill now." He still had authority. His dismissal obviously hadn't occurred—yet.

The steward was creating favor with his lord's debtors. He had just eradicated a huge portion of their debt, so he could now go to them and ask for a favor. He had created favor with these men, and truly believed they would help him. The steward was ingenious. He had resolve.

"So the master commended the unjust steward because he had dealt shrewdly. For the sons of this world are more shrewd in their generation than the sons of light." (v. 8). This is an important verse. Jesus transitioned and made his point here. Let's start with the first part of the verse. The steward's master was impressed with his resolve to position himself in the best possible way for his financial recovery. His plan, mixed with resolve, was bringing him favor, and a possible future job with the men who owed his master. He now had a few allies that would help him. The discounts he offered were a tremendous favor to the debtors. He was well-positioned for recovery.

Looking now at the second part of the verse, we see Jesus saying, "For the sons of this world are more shrewd in their generation than the sons of light." Ouch. What Jesus was saying is "The people in the world honor and hear their god, *money*, more than My children heed Me." That hurts. But it's true.

It takes resolve on our part to follow Holy Spirit's instructions. Notice how quickly the steward acted. He didn't hesitate, because he knew his time was limited. If he didn't act quickly, he was out of the window of opportunity. I wonder why we don't see God's instructions to us, or a word of Scripture, the same way?

Jesus stated that the world's wisdom comes because they act

quickly on the instructions their god—you know, money—gives them. They plan, plot, think, and consider their moves to make money. What would happen if we did what the world does in wanting to follow our Father? I wonder how quickly we could win the lost, save the broken, and heal the sick? Again, being about our Father's business.

"And I say to you, make friends for yourselves by unrighteous mammon, that when you fail, they may receive you into an everlasting home" (v. 9). Here is another very debatable, hard-to-understand verse. What if we follow God in a thing like making money? What if we could get His perspective on it as a tool and not a god? Then we could get an eternal view of what God wants to do. We could make the money, use it to win souls, and do God's work.

When we die and go to heaven, we would get the reward for all of the born-again people. In other words, the evangelists get their reward for preaching and getting people saved. The intercessors get their reward for praying in the people who got saved. And the person who financed the crusade, paid the preachers' and intercessors' salaries, from the money they made in this world, get the same reward.

"He who is faithful in *what* is least is faithful also in much: and he who is unjust in what is least is unjust also in much" (v. 10). Pretty simple here. The small things bring on big things. If you do what is *at hand* to do, God will give you more. When we are faithful, following and praying for people as He asks us, our faith grows. As our faith grows, we know and trust Him. In that trusting and stronger faith, it is much easier to do the miracles of God.

This verse is pivotal as well. It is why some receive and some don't. It is why some live by faith and others are in a grace-and-mercy place. No condemnation. We are learning to follow our Father and learn how the kingdom works. Let's be about our Father's business and learn. It doesn't matter how old or young we are. We need to learn from Him.

There's much more in Luke 16 about being double-minded compared to single-minded. Jesus speaks further about honoring God over money. In other words, being single to God's instructions. If you are called to handle money and you obey God's instructions, doing it His way, you get the money without it owning you.

I want us to understand the level of resolve the unjust steward walked in. If we could walk in this same level of resolve in following God's instructions, we would attain what He wants for our lives. I want us to go from His instructions being an option, to His instructions being *life*. I want us to go to the place where His instructions are how we move and live in Him—and where His instructions deserve our resolve.

PARTNERSHIP – BEING ABOUT OUR FATHER'S BUSINESS

W e have covered a lot in this book. Even so, I want us to see that there is always more in God. He is an ever-infinite source of life, wisdom, and knowledge. His goal is to save this dying world. He is after every generation to win them and to get them to know who He is. He wants none of us to perish but for all to find life (see 2 Peter 3:9).

He also sees our potential and is wanting more from us. He wants more people He can call His children. He wants more of our time, more of our awareness, more of our fellowship, and—I believe strongly—He wants to be able to depend on us. To depend on us to partner with Him and to be about our Father's business. To get this world saved and translated from the kingdom of darkness to the kingdom of His dear Son.

If we look back, Genesis 18:16–33 speaks of God's plan to destroy Sodom and Gomorrah because of the sin that was so overwhelmingly prevalent. This city was so vile that God decided to erase it from the face of the earth. That had to be a heart-wrenching decision. But before He did, He decided to counsel with His servant and friend, Abraham. "I mean to destroy an entire culture" is a huge decision. I still find it interesting that the Creator wanted to consult a man. A man He did trust.

Abraham had developed his faith to the point that he was dependable in matters of leading God's family. But I believe we need to see that it was a faith that grew by experience. Experience comes by not only learning how to do something, but also by learning how *not* to do something. No way around it, learning to walk with God will have highs and lows. It is our job to continue in the faith, learning to not waver and say it doesn't work—or, worse yet—blame God.

Part of growing up in Him is learning how God operates and how God looks at situations. I believe our Father is always for us and does all He can to help us. We have a choice. We are the ones who decide to walk, or not walk, single-minded to His eternal instructions.

Let's look at a verse from this passage in Genesis 18: "And the Lord said, Shall I hide from Abraham [My friend and servant] what I am going to do" (v. 17). There's a lot to cover here, and I'm going to share something that isn't considered much in today's Christian community. We are, however, as a body of believers, getting to the point where we're open to the things of heaven operating more on this earth. But for the naysayers, no, we aren't God. But yes, we can partner with God. So please just consider this. All I ask. Please ask Holy Spirit what He thinks, if this is an issue for you.

In verse 17, God calls Abraham his friend. I personally believe that being a friend of someone is the highest place we can be in human interaction. Friends choose to be with each other, consult and share with each other, and live life with each other. It is a mutual agreement. I believe it is the highest compliment we can give to someone. The dictionary defines a friend as follows: "a person whom one knows and with whom one has a bond of mutual affection, typically exclusive of sexual or family relations."[1]

I feel like I'm covering a well-known area of human interaction when I share with everyone reading this book about friendship. We all know it, right? But let's consider a few things. I have seen, as have you, relationships that are extremely close. Two people who are not part of a family or related in any way but choose to trust and fellowship with each other. Sometimes, they are closer to this person than they are to their own family. It's a relationship built on trust, reliance, experience, and, in most cases, is free of judgment. A safe place, in other words.

The use of *friend* here is not the same as a social media friend. It's not someone who takes our friend request without really knowing us, but someone who knows us intimately.

The church has preached about sonship, covenant, and relationship for years. My pastor, a few years back, spoke of *fellowship* as being the highest place in God. He defined fellowship as when two people choose to spend time together. These two people are choosing to get to know each other on an intimate level. Not necessarily as a romantic thing, but in a place of safety and expression. It's an interesting dynamic.

This is the very reason I believe that walking with God in friendship and fellowship is the highest place we can attain. Again, my opinion. But I've seen relatives who do not fellowship with each other. I've seen fathers and sons not talk or fellowship with each other for years. But at the same time, both of those men have close friends who they speak with and see on a daily basis. These friends they have chosen are as close to them, or closer, than their own family.

Here's an interesting thought: We are part of God's family, and He wants to spend all the time with us that we can possibly give Him. To me, that isn't always locked up in prayer, though I have spent many nights and days fellowshipping in a room with Him. I believe there is a stronger place than that.

What is that place? Awareness. Awareness of Him. Awareness that I am fellowshipping with Him no matter what I'm doing or where I am.

I don't believe it only has to be a physical place or time,

though I do cherish locking up with Him for days on end. I see it as a continual, daily, moment-by-moment lifestyle choice. No matter what we're doing or where we are, we are aware of Him. We already know He is aware of us. We're just learning to act like Him, be like Him, and be aware like He is.

This is how Jesus did it. He was always aware of His Father. His Father's awareness was the strongest reality in Jesus's life. That awareness was the gateway to His being able to access the Father. To go boldly into the throne room of grace (see Hebrews 4:16). He was also able to hear from Father. Look at this absolutely amazing passage in the book of John:

I can of mine own self do nothing: as I hear, I judge: and my judgment is just; because I seek not mine own will, but the will of the Father which hath sent me. If I bear witness of myself, my witness is not true. There is another that beareth witness of me, and I know that the witness which he witnesseth of me is true. (John 5:30–32 KJV)

Are you seeing what Jesus was saying? Look at verse 30. He did nothing by Himself. He was asking His Father what to do—what was required. He was friends with His Father. Yes, Jesus is God's Son, but He is the Father's friend as well.

In the rest of this verse, Jesus was saying that He only consults the Father, that He only judges and decides to do what His Father is telling Him. That He doesn't judge anything by what it looks like on this earth. Jesus does as the Father instructs. That is all He needs. What the Father thinks is all that matters.

This passage shows us, early in Jesus' life, how He understood this partnership between Himself and His Father. Even earlier in His life, an obvious reference to this partnership was the twelve-year-old Jesus who was about His Father's business (see Luke 2:41–50). Many of us still haven't comprehended what He was saying there. When we see it, and we will, our lives will change forever. We are to be about what our Father wants on this earth.

To single-mindedly follow our Father. The way of safety. The way of peace. The way of partnership.

Continuing in John 5: "If I bear witness of myself, my witness is not true" (v. 31 KJV). Talk about friendship, partnership, and sonship. Jesus essentially says, "You can't even see Me or discern Me without My Father's opinion. In fact, I don't even decide what I am or what I look like. I depend on my Father to tell me that. And remember, and do not mistake this, Father is the senior partner. He is God. We will never be equal. He is Lord. We are sons."

If that isn't a partnership, I don't know what is. Consider this: When we read in Scripture what it says we are, does our opinion really matter? I mean, we can determine if we're going to follow what Scripture says or not. We can decide to believe Scripture or not. We have free will, after all. But there is a place where we trust someone enough that we honor what they tell us. This is what the Father is trying to do for us.

He wants us to see ourselves the way He sees us. His opinion is much higher than ours. Scripture is loaded with His promises for us. But to access them, we need to see ourselves the way Jesus did in this last verse. There is more we can attain. Much more.

Moving on to verse 32: "There is another that beareth witness of me, and I know that the witness which he witnesseth of me is true" (KJV). This verse is telling us to honor the witness of our Father. To see ourselves the way Father does. This is a huge leap of faith for us. This world and society have dictated to us who we're supposed to be. Our family and relatives have dictated who we're supposed to be. We've dictated what we thought we should be. And we have that right. We have free will. But I'll ask a simple question: Will we ever let the Father's opinion of us become stronger than our own?

Consider a partnership where you work in conjunction with someone in building an entity. This goes on in businesses, medical practices, legal practices, and companies, just to give a few examples. Some in the business world now use the term *joint venture*. The point is this, there is power in partnering with people. And it is much better to partner with someone who is better at something than we are. They, in turn, receive the benefits of our strength too. It can be a wonderful thing when it works. If egos and selfishness can stay out of the mix, the benefits can last for years.

Is it too hard a thing to see that God wants to partner with us on this earth? Are we able to handle that? Or do we stay in our self-limiting beliefs? Are we destined to continually fight off problems and barely get along in this life? You know, suffer through and get our rewards when we get to glory. We should want a life of pleasing our Father. We're supposed to be overcomers in *this* life.

Now look at Amos 3:3: "Can two walk together, except they agree?" (KJV). This is a powerful, thought-provoking verse. We can't really walk as He wants us to until we agree with His position. Grace and mercy are available for when we go our own way and get in a precarious situation, but to partner—and I mean really partner—don't we need to get on board with His plans? And again, the main emphasis for Jesus coming to the cross was to 1) love God, 2) love our fellow man, and 3) seek and save those who are lost.

The Father's business is souls. It is soul-winning. It is spreading His love to all people. The position of always needing help, and not seeing what Jesus did for us on the cross, is a place of not being able to help others. This helping others is to seek the lost whom Jesus came to save.

Are we too drama-filled with our "stuff" to do our part in the "family business"? Are we too concerned with our doctrinal position to care for a dying world? Are we way too concerned about ourselves and our own comfort to be about helping Heavenly Father?

Partnerships are built on trust—on the ability of both partners to complete the task at hand. As I looked up *partnership* for this book, the dictionary led me to other words. The word *partnership* evolved from the word *partake*. The word *partake* opened a plethora of places in the Bible to study.

But let me leave it at this: I want to partake in my Father's business. I want to help bring heaven to earth. I want to be the solution and not the drama-filled problem. Concerning what I've done in this earthly life, I want to hear my heavenly Father say, "Well done." That is enough. That is more than enough.

I'll finish this chapter with the same passage we studied earlier in John 5, this time from *THE MESSAGE*:

"I can't do a solitary thing on my own: I listen, then I decide. You can trust my decision because I'm not out to get my own way but only to carry out orders. If I were simply speaking on my own account, it would be an empty, self-serving witness. But an independent witness confirms me, the most reliable Witness of all." (vv. 30–32)

A FINAL THOUGHT

I want to sum up this book with a final thought about our Father and being single-minded. In His kind generosity, He has laid out a plan for us to follow. He wants us to believe Him. He knew life on this earth would be hard at times. He wants to help us get through this life with as much of His leadership as possible. He says that He gives us a way of escape from the snares the Enemy throws at us.

But in order to attain that, there's another pivotal verse that we have to make a working part of our lives: "But without faith it is impossible to please him: for he that cometh to God must believe that he is and that he is a rewarder of them that diligently seek him" (Hebrews 11:6 KJV). This verse is the answer to how to overcome in this world, and to do so right in the middle of our life journey. It's one of those verses that must be considered in depth to adequately interpret.

I like the verse. I believe it is a foundational piece that helps us have a true, non-religious understanding of God and His character. I want to break the verse down in detail so we can understand it fully, as I believe what I've written in this book hinges on this verse as well as Mark 4:13. I believe that faith springs from both of these verses.

Hebrews 11:6 has four conditional stipulations. The first part of the verse says "but without faith, it is impossible to please him." Simple enough. He is a faith-God. On our part, we activate faith with a renewed mind. A mind that falls in line with what Scripture or our Father personally tells us. In other words, being single-minded to what is being said.

But more importantly, we serve a God who operates only by faith. He does not consider any other way. When we don't use faith, we are in a place of double-mindedness to His will. It is difficult to get an answer to our problems when we don't follow His instructions. Real faith comes by following Him fully. Another word we can use is *surrender*. We are surrendering our will to His. His instructions are the starting line, and that's the best place I can think of to begin.

The second part of the verse says "for he that cometh to God." Simple enough here as well. We have to come to Him. We have to approach Him. He can only move on our behalf if we come to Him. We receive little from God otherwise. We are His children, and He wants us to come to Him for guidance and help. He never meant for us to do life on our own. In Mark 5, the demoniac of the Gaderenes saw Jesus coming from far off and ran to him for help. No one else ever helped him. He knew Jesus had the answer. He came to God by coming to Jesus.

The prodigal son came back to his father. His father was at home waiting for his son to return. Waiting to help his son. We have to do the same. We have to come to God. We have to come home as the prodigal did. The woman with the issue of blood tried everything she could think of to get healed. She spent all of her money on doctors. Scripture says she even got worse. But the day came when she decided to come to God. That is the key here. We have to come to God.

Part three of the verse says "must believe that he is." Let's skip this section for a moment since we're going to spend most of the rest of this chapter on this part of the verse.

Part four is really awesome: "and that he is a rewarder of

them that diligently seek Him." I like that. He rewards us when we diligently seek Him. A very simple instruction. *Reward* is defined as "a thing given in recognition of one's service, effort, or achievement."[1] So a *rewarder* would be someone who gives out rewards. *Diligent* is defined as "characterized by steady, earnest, and energetic effort."[2]

This portion of the verse is saying that as we come to Him, seeking with all our heart, He then rewards us. This is the truth. Outside the realm of mercy, it is difficult for Him to reward us without our diligently seeking Him. He gives us what we need to seek Him though. He isn't going to leave us on our own. He will help us do this, but we have to come with our attention fully focused on Him. Single-minded again. There is no other way to do this.

This verse is the key to stability in our lives. Stability comes when we single-mindedly focus on the things that are said to us in the Word. We stop trying to create stability from the outside natural realm. We stop attempting to find stability by trying to change outside circumstances and trying to get them to line up with our desires. We see that stability comes from God taking part in our problem, instructing us through our problem, and holding our hand until the end. Then the external circumstance conforms to His will and not ours.

Look at the New Life Version of Hebrews 11:6: "A man cannot please God unless he has faith. Anyone who comes to God must believe that He is. That one must also know that God gives what is promised to the one who *keeps on looking for Him.*"

We are not necessarily going to Him just to have Him fix the problem. But we are simply seeking Him for instructions. Then, those instructions, followed out single-mindedly, will help us get through and solve the problem.

Now let's go back to the third stipulation of this verse: "must believe that he is." What is really being said here? When I believe He is real, and I mean truly believe it, I can go boldly into the throne room of grace and ask for what I need. I can take His wonderful voice, a passage of Scripture, or an inner leading, and operate and move in it. I can, as the financial world says, "bank on it." Think about that. It is a 100 percent guarantee. If we fall short of that guarantee, we always have a loving God who covers us in mercy. But we need to learn His ways.

Isn't this real grace? I've heard people say that they no longer have to work because Jesus did it all for us at the cross. I agree. But consider that problems still come our way. We need a way to escape. Since Jesus made a way of escape, we're going to capitalize off His grace and get instructions for overcoming the problem. I'm not teaching works.

A friend of mine living in California shared one of his life experiences from many years back. He was in a horrific motorcycle accident, and when the accident occurred, he was not serving God. He was struck by a truck head-on when the vehicle entered his lane. My friend was catapulted off the motorcycle into the air, and he landed hard on the pavement, which caused tremendous trauma and injury.

His pelvic bone was broken in many places. He sustained multiple other broken bones and injuries. Due to the critical nature of his injuries, the doctors felt he had little chance of surviving. The surgeon wasn't in a hurry to operate. Their knowledge of the human body said the trauma my friend had suffered was not repairable. They decided to sedate him to stop the pain and let him pass away.

Eight days later, when it looked like he would survive, they decided to send him to another hospital for surgery. The doctors said to my friend, "Your bones are kneading together in the wrong place. They are kneading according to the fractures." So without delay, they took him into the operating room.

During the preop, as the surgeons prepared outside the room, an amazing thing happened: Jesus walked through the wall into that room. My friend, not a Christian yet, talked with Jesus. He visited with my friend alone before surgery. Jesus came to give him a message: He hadn't given up on him. This man had work to do in God's kingdom. He just didn't know it yet because he wasn't born again. He didn't know how to pray. He had no concept of God and His kingdom. He was lost.

I believe someone had to have been praying for him. Who knows who it was. Someone who God had quickened to rescue my friend from a life of debauchery, and ultimately hell. Don't tell me God doesn't answer someone else's prayer for us.

Listen to what Jesus said to him: "Man can't heal you, but I will. I want you to tell people I am real. Most people think I'm an ethereal being. They don't know that I am a real person. They think of me and treat me as if I am Casper the Friendly Ghost." Jesus shared much more with my friend, but I believe this is enough to make my point. People sometimes struggle with God being real. They struggle with God truly caring for them.

When our lives are invaded by a hard problem, we can be unstable. When real trouble comes into our life, many of us fall apart. But I believe we are in a season where our Father is revealing Himself to more and more people. The reality of His being real should start to become obvious to the body of Christ. I believe God is saving the best for last.

As a side note, my friend recovered in a few months. Medical science had given up on him, but Jesus hadn't. My friend is alive and sharing the gospel today. The accident occurred in January 1986. Since then, he has never doubted the validity of God being alive. He has an experience with God, not a theory. We really do need to experience God. No more doubt and second-guessing. No more wondering if He will help us. No more concern about His caring.

Believing that God is real is vitally important for us to establish our faith. Believing that He is *our* rewarder is just as important. We have to believe that He has our best interests in mind. He knows how to get us through this life much better than we do. Consider Him as our manufacturer. Did the Creator make us? Yes, so why don't we let a *factory recall* happen in our lives? Why don't we go back to the manufacturer and get a tune-up?

How about living in a permanent place of being *tuned up* daily. A place where He is looking out for us and directing us in a very personal way.

While I was teaching in a strong, charismatic church a few years back, the Lord said to me, "Have an altar call for the people who don't believe I am real." My immediate response was, "No. I'm not doing that. These people are from the buckle on the Bible Belt. These people have moved from all over the United States to come to church here. These people *know* you are real."

Well, if you know anything about the Lord, He doesn't change His mind. He isn't going to change His mind over our doubt-filled conclusions—or, as I like to say, our double-mindedness.

I stood at the altar for a few minutes, debating what I had been instructed to do by Holy Spirit. Many thoughts rolled through my mind. Thoughts like, *I'll never preach here again. I will be ostracized. I will be kicked out of the ministry. I'll never get another place to preach. I'm about to tell a faith-filled, tongue-talking charismatic church that some in the congregation don't believe. I mean, really believe that He is real.*

Maybe I should rephrase it this way: There were times when the people in this church had doubted of God's existence. There were times when they weren't sure if He would move on their behalf. Would He truly help them out of their problems? Maybe worry and doubt had replaced peace and answers. Should we assume that since we are strong in God in one area, we are close to Him in all areas?

So I took a leap of faith. I remember having the resolve of a soaked poodle after a severe thunderstorm. I sheepishly said, "If you don't believe that God is real...or you have moments where you doubt He really exists...come up here to the altar."

There. I'd said it! I was obedient to Him. I still felt strongly that I would suffer the consequences of saying it, though. Thoughts bombarded my mind: *I'll be back in the secular world in no*

*time. Back to my old marketing job. No one invites a preacher who
insults the congregation.*

To my worst fear, no one came up to the altar. I knew it. I
missed it. I missed God! Then a lady moved *slowly* out of her
seat. One honest lady answered the call and came up. Then
another honest person came up—again, slowly. But then something started happening. More and more people started coming
forward. The altar was starting to fill up. People fell down under
the power as they came up. His presence filled the altar. People
started crying and calling out to God. He started proving to us
that He was real. I think at one point there were as many people
at the altar as were still sitting in their seats. Fifty percent of the
people came forward! Fifty percent!

What I found interesting was that this was a Wednesday-
night service. This was "the serious service," when the really
committed Christians came out—the ones who wanted to be
single-minded, the ones who wanted to fast and pray. This wasn't
the Sunday-morning crowd. You know, the ones who come
because it's the thing to do. What would have happened on a
Sunday morning? How many would have come up then?

I'm saying all this to re-emphasize the point. We have to
believe He is real. We have to know Him as Rewarder. We have
to know Him as our Father. We need to know Him as our
Problem Solver. We have to know Him as our Single-Minded
Source. How do we do that? What is the secret sauce? What is
the magic pill we can take that gets us to the point that we
believe that the Father really is real?

I'll share the simplest, easiest way to do it. This method has
always brought me results. My secret is... (drum roll, please)...
spending time with Him. That's it. Whomever we spend our
time with is whom we will become like. It is the law of associa-
tion. The people we associate with are the people we become
like. We literally start to think and process as they do.

So, to process and learn to think like God, it seems we would
give Him all the time we can. From this place of giving Him

time, we learn to associate and become aware of Him as we walk throughout our day. We grow hungry enough to become aware of Him. Spending time with Him teaches us to be aware of His presence. This awareness starts to be *more real* to us than the problem and situations we are facing. This awareness of God is what Jesus walked in. It is the reason He was so successful in ministry. Paul did it. Smith Wigglesworth did it. Kenneth Hagin did it. Charles Finney did it. We should learn from these great men of God.

So learning more about God and how He thinks is a serendipity of spending time with Him. Spending time with Him settles the debate of His being real. Spending time with Him settles the debate of His loving us. It settles the debate of His doing something for us. It settles the debate of His healing power working for us and working for others as we pray for them.

It also settles this debate in our mind. In other words, it stops the double-mindedness we walk in. We start to see that He is real, He loves us, and He is for us. We can now get single-minded to that truth only. We begin to walk in the land of stability.

We also discover that He thinks a certain way. His timing is better than ours. He is never late, He is never forgetful, and He is never negligent. We start to see that God gets blamed for a lot of things that He has nothing to do with. We start to see that people who blame God for their tragedies really don't know Him very well. If we don't spend time following Him and getting to know Him, we really can't blame Him when things don't go our way.

When we first start to spend time with Him, it is usually about getting our needs met, solving our problems, and God being our immediate help in a time of need. This is what I call the infant-adolescent stage. He is our Father. He cares for us like little children. Remember the Scripture that says we must come to Him like little children (see Matthew 18:3)? Enjoy this stage. It is a real growing time in Him. But we must move on. We have to get about our Father's business. There are souls to be born again. That is our responsibility.

The next place is the place of presence. We are growing up in Him. We are now experiencing worship and the anointings of God. This is the place where we're still coming to Him for our needs but are now getting His instructions. It's the place of ministry and helping others. It may even be the place of strong fellowship. It is a good place. But we need to move on. There is still more to do and learn from Him.

The place that I see so few attain is the place of fellowship. Constant fellowship. A place where we are no longer looking at His hand. You know, asking, "What can He do for me? What can He do in my church service? What can He do for me and my ministry?" It's the place where we truly know that *He has me.* We know He knows our needs, desires, and dreams. This is the place where we stop taking control. Where we don't talk so much or barrage Him with questions. This is the place where we know we have a lot to say and bring to the table, but we let Him talk and have control. We stop achieving and trying and simply let Him be God. We let Him tell us who we are. We're giving Him our identity. So much so that we're going to use our faith to the utmost extreme—to rest in Him totally. That's right. Just sitting and *being.*

The next phase, or final position, on this earth is the realm where He just takes us. We have become so much more of a heavenly being than an earthly being that we just go with Him. Bringing heaven to earth is as natural as walking down the street. This is the place where Enoch lived. It is an indescribable place of bliss. This to me is the quest we all truly would like to attain. We see everything from the heavenly perspective. Earth has faded away. To be taken by God. Wow.

In order to be in His perfect will, there is another secret. To be in the place of perfect peace, there is a formula. It is doing what he tells us to do. It's that simple. This is a place of no striving. A place of resting. A place of peace. A place of total reliance on Him. It is the place of losing reliance on ourselves.

Smith Wigglesworth said, "If there is a thing God wants to do today, He wants to be as real to you and me as He was to Abraham."[3] This is where the partnership with Him comes into play. Where we are now dependable and God has no problem consulting with us. Abraham lived here. Can you imagine the living God asking your opinion? That is what He did with Abraham. And he was an old-covenant man. We are in the new covenant. A much better covenant and position in Him.

My goal is not to be controversial. My goal is to share the truth. The truth that we are more than conquerors. The truth that we can live a victorious life. The truth that we can win this generation and stop them from going to hell. The truth that we are world changers. A truth that we need to grasp.

We are God's children. He cares about us and loves us. He believes we will do what He has asked of us, and He is waiting for us to believe that too.

AFTERWORD

A few points about what I've covered in this book. My hope is that we achieve these milestones in our lives.

1) Learn to know God and who He is. We do that by spending as much time with Him as we possibly can. Read His Word—the Bible—daily. Learn to know His voice. Learn to know His ways. Also, learn to take all that He has prepared for us. A great way to start is by getting the baptism in the Holy Ghost. Getting the nature of God—the "new nature." The world has the nature of "the self." I want the nature of God.

2) By learning to do step one, we learn that God is real. That debate no longer exists in our mind. We are now able to find Him for ourselves. We have experienced Him because we give Him our time. Nothing we do in this life is as important as time with God. Nothing. So the debate of there being a God who cares for us is now over. Remember, the proof of this is the level of patience and peace we walk in. If God is our Father, He won't leave us fatherless. Fear and doubt are signs we don't believe this.

3) We now learn to hear Him. I mean truly hear Him. Since we know He is real, we have the confidence to do what He has told us. Remember the Scripture verse we shared in the last chapter, Hebrews 11:6. Having a true reality in our lives shows

that we aren't caught up in a theory. Theories now become just that: a theory. Not a theory our friend shared with us concerning what they think we should be doing. Not a theory our spouse may bring to us. Or, the most dangerous of all, what our own mindset brings to us. We hopefully get past this point in our life. We depend on God. We *know* we hear God. We become stable.

4) We now become single-minded to step three. We follow those instructions with great regard for our Father. We have found the "pearl of great price" (see Matthew 13:46). It is a treasure. It is full of light and life. What is it again? His instructions to us. So stay single-minded to those simple instructions.

5) We learn to stop being double-minded. We learn to stop going our own way and second-guessing what Holy Spirit is telling us. We no longer give ourselves options outside of what we have been instructed by God. We stay away from guilt, fear, condemnation, arrogance, self-innovation, etc. We see that we are spiritual beings. We operate as our Father does. We are learning to operate as Jesus did. We don't waver from our divine instructions.

6) We stop the winning-and-losing stage of our lives. We are no longer moved by what we see, hear, or feel—or by what we don't understand. We are moved only by faith in God. We hear and we follow. We are moved only by our Father, and the thing that moves us is Holy Spirit's instructions. The outcome of the problem no longer moves us. It no longer matters if it turns out good or bad. We are acting according to what Father tells us, regardless of whether we understand, our neighbor understands, or our best friends understand. It is now in the realm of faith.

7) Finally, we learn to rest. Having done all to stand, we stand (see Ephesians 6:13). Rest. Just simple, powerful, all-fulfilling rest. Like how Jesus did at the back of the boat during that horrific storm. Rest. Because the instructions from heaven, the instructions from Scripture, are *more real* to us than the circumstances we are surrounded by. We rest in the instructions. We rest the way the Creator did after He created this earth.

This is just the beginning. Holy Spirit has loaded me up with many more books on this subject. There will be other books that expound upon the various chapters in this book. We are told that God has inexhaustible riches. Join me in this quest. Let's go find a few of those divine riches before we leave this planet.

I like what a friend shared with me one day by text. If I do nothing else on this earth, texts like this are why I'm here.

I have realized that I have spent my whole life attempting to follow and serve God without much reality to my relationship with Him. I have learned more in the last 9 months than the combined nearly 50 years... the "I know" has almost completely left... not that knowledge is not relevant but if the expression of my current level of knowledge blocks the attaining of further revelation then why would I do that? Father already knows what I know and what I don't. Why would I want to be a mouthy teenager in my relationship with God? That is what I was in April.

Father really does know best. Maturity in our relationship with God is not demonstrated by how much knowledge we have accumulated but by how deep a relationship we have cultivated. I thank God every day for allowing me to really get to know Him! You have been so instrumental in that and I thank Him every day for you as well! Thank you for letting Him use you as He does. Thank you for letting Him change you and rearrange you so He can flow through you. Thank you for learning to love. Thank you for letting me see not only your strength but also your struggles. Thank you!

Let us hear the conclusion of the whole matter:
Fear God, and keep his commandments:
for this is the whole duty of man.
(Ecclesiastes 12:13 KJV)

SCRIPTURE INDEX

Chapter 5: Mark 4:35–41; Luke 8:22–25; Genesis 3:6; James 1:2–4; Mark 4:36–37; John 4:40; 1 John 4:17; Deuteronomy 31:6; Hebrews 13:5

Chapter 7: 2 Chronicles 17:6; 20:1–4; 1 John 4:24; Proverbs 16:7

Chapter 8: Matthew 6:22; James 1:8; 1 John 2:9; John 16:13; James 1:2–8; Isaiah 53; John 12; Joshua 24:14; Romans 12:1; John 1:5–7; Psalm 119:105; Jeremiah 29:11

Chapter 9: James 1:2; Hebrews 12:2; James 1:3–4; John 11:9; James 1:5–6; Hebrews 11:6; Mark 4; James 1:7; Romans 14:23; James 1:8; Isaiah 26:3

Chapter 10: Romans 2:4; Romans 12:10; 1 John 4:20

Chapter 11: John 14:15; John 14:21; John 14:23–24; 1 Peter 1:19–20; Exodus 20:1–17; Matthew 22:36–40; Matthew 24:35; 1 John 4:20–21; James 1:7–8; Matthew 5:43–48

Chapter 12: Hebrews 12:1–4; Hebrews 11; Luke 16:1–10

Chapter 13: 2 Peter 3:9; Genesis 18:16–33; Hebrews 4:16; John 5:30–32; Amos 3:3

Chapter 14: Hebrews 11:6; Mark 4:13; Mark 5; Matthew 18:3

Conclusion: Matthew 13:46; Ephesians 6:13; Ecclesiastes 12:13

NOTES

11. IT ALL WORKS BY LOVE

1. "Mourners honor Mother Teresa at funeral Mass," *CNN*, September 13, 1997, http://edition.cnn.com/WORLD/9709/13/teresa.service/index.html.

12. RESOLVE

1. Maurice Waite and Christine A. Lindberg, *Pocket Oxford American Dictionary and Thesaurus* (Oxford, UK: Oxford University Press, 2010), 666.
2. *Vocabulary.com*, s.v. "resolve," https://www.vocabulary.com/dictionary/resolve#:-:text=As%20a%20noun%2C%20resolve%20refers,to%20stick%20with%20your%20program.

13. PARTNERSHIP – BEING ABOUT OUR FATHER'S BUSINESS

1. Kris Evans, "On Friendship," *HuffPost*, September 29, 2013, https://www.huffpost.com/entry/on-friendship_b_3671681#:-:text=The%20dictionary%20describes%20a%20friend,relationship%20less%20intimate%20than%20friendship.

14. A FINAL THOUGHT

1. *Lexico*, s.v. "reward," https://www.lexico.com/definition/reward.
2. *Merriam-Webster.com Dictionary*, s.v. "diligent," https://www.merriam-webster.com/dictionary/diligent.
3. Smith Wigglesworth, *The Power of Faith* (New Kensington, PA: Whitaker House, 2000).

Made in USA - Kendallville, IN
1163021_9780578237060
02.23.2021 1606